THE WONDERWORLD OF SCIENCE

By
WARREN KNOX
GEORGE STONE
MORRIS MEISTER
DOROTHY WHEATLEY
·
Illustrated by
ALMA FRODERSTROM
SYD OXBERRY
FRANK HUBBARD

Book Six

CHARLES SCRIBNER'S SONS · NEW YORK

CHICAGO · BOSTON · ATLANTA · SAN FRANCISCO · DALLAS

PREFACE

The world of science constitutes an integral part of the whole environment which must be made meaningful to children in our elementary schools. Learning in science must, therefore, become an integral part of the elementary school curriculum. This book is planned as one of a series which presents a well articulated program of learning experiences in science. The program is not only well balanced with respect to all phases of the natural environment but also planned as a functional part of the whole elementary school curriculum. It will give meaning, enrichment, and added significance to other areas of learning such as safety and health, the social studies, mathematics, the language arts and the fine arts.

The Wonderworld of Science series is designed to be used as basal textbooks. Good textbooks should stimulate pupils to perform experiments, to engage in individual and group projects, to make field trips, to read other science books, and to carry on other worthwhile activities. The series represents a careful selection of appropriate experiences rather than an attempt at encyclopedic abridgement of scientific knowledge. The careful construction and interest appeal make it excellent material for general reading purposes.

The authors gratefully acknowledge the whole-hearted cooperation furnished by teachers and supervisors in rural and urban schools in the experimentation with and the critical analysis of the materials that make up this book.

The Authors

CONTENTS

FOOD FOR GROWTH AND ENERGY

WEATHER AND CLIMATE

ELECTRICITY AND ITS USES

THE WORLD OF SOUND

WONDERS OF THE SKY

THE IMPROVEMENT OF PLANTS AND ANIMALS

KEEPING FIT FOR WORK AND PLAY

FOOD FOR GROWTH AND ENERGY

Animals and Their Food

Mountain goats spend most of their time looking for food. Food gives them energy. They use this energy to move about in search for more food.

Mountain goats are not the only animals that eat food in order to have energy to obtain more food. If we watch the activities of different kinds of animals we will find that nearly all of them are kept busy solving their food problem. In fact, for most of them, life is a constant struggle for food.

Some kinds of animals obtain their food directly from green plants. Others get their food from animals that eat green plants. Green plants make the food for all the living things on earth.

Animals secure food in thousands of different ways. Though several kinds of animals eat the same kind of food, each animal seems to have its own way of obtaining it. Animals that eat grass, for instance, differ widely in their eating habits. Horses take the grass between their teeth and pull backwards. The sharp edges of their upper teeth help to tear off the grass. While grazing, a cow places her lower jaw near the ground in front of the grass. She then pushes her tongue around the grass and closes her mouth. By a forward push of the jaw, she cuts off the grass. Sheep eat grass in very much the same way that cows do, but they cut off the grass much shorter.

Ants serve as food for many kinds of animals. Flickers and other birds are often seen thrusting their beaks into ant hills. The larvae of tiger beetles make small holes in the ground and close the entrances of the holes with their heads. Then, with their bodies hidden in the holes, they wait for ants to walk by. If an ant happens to cross over one of these holes, it is seized by the strong jaws of the larvae. Anteaters break open ant hills and catch the helpless ants with their long sticky tongues.

Woodpeckers may often be seen on the sides of trees, sounding the trunks with their bills. They are looking for insects in the wood or under the bark. When a woodpecker locates such an insect, it pecks a hole in the tree and eats the insect.

Some animals catch all of their food on the wing. Bats are very awkward on the ground, but while flying they catch large numbers of mosquitoes. Dragonflies, too, are excellent flyers; they are able to remain stationary in the air while waiting for an insect to come near. When one appears, they dart toward it and soon overtake it. Flycatchers and some other birds also feed while flying.

Animals have many different ways of catching fish. Raccoons hide along the shore and catch fish with their front paws. Kingfishers perch on limbs over the water, swoop and seize

the fish in their powerful bills and fly away with them. Pelicans dive into the water and catch fish with their large bills. Diving beetles swim up to fish and fasten their feet among the scales. Then they pierce a hole in the fish with their beaks and draw out the blood.

Gulls use their feet to pick up clams along the shore. Since a gull is not able to open a clam, it sometimes carries it into the air and drops it on a rock. This usually breaks the shell of the clam. If it does not, the gull again picks up the clam and drops it from a greater height. As soon as the shell is broken, the clam is easy to eat.

Clams, oysters and mussels have a very interesting way of eating. Their food consists of tiny water plants and animals, many of which are too small to be seen. A clam draws in water through a tube called a siphon. It strains out the food that is in the water and forces the water out through another tube, or siphon. A clam of average size removes food from about thirty gallons of water each day.

A single drop of pond water may contain many kinds of tiny animals. One kind that is often present is the ameba, which has a very simple way of obtaining food. When an ameba meets something that is good to eat, it seems to surround the food particle and thus force the food into its body.

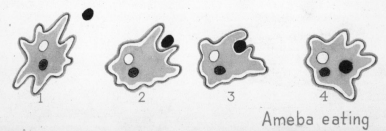

Ameba eating

1   2   3   4

Amebas are the simplest of all animals. An ameba does not have any eyes, mouth, stomach, feet or head. It is just a tiny speck of living Ameba matter consisting of a single cell. It takes in dividing food directly from the water in which it lives, and gives off waste products into the same water. The food that it eats gives it energy to move and secure more food. Some of the food is also used to help the ameba to grow. When an ameba grows to a certain size, it divides into two parts, and then there are two amebas.

Besides amebas, hundreds of other kinds of one-celled animals live in the waters of streams, rivers, lakes and oceans. Beautiful bell-shaped animals called vorticella are fastened by long stalks to water weeds. The bell part of the animal serves as a mouth. Vorticella move by coiling and uncoiling the stalk part. Other

Vorticella

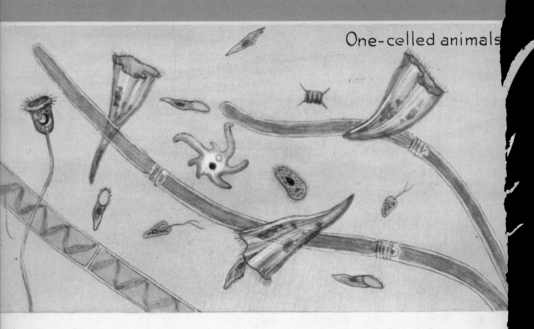

tiny animals move about in search of food by means of moving hair-like organs which cover their bodies. The hairs work like oars in pushing these tiny animals through the water.

Besides the one-celled animals, tiny animals of many cells are also found in water. They can easily be seen with a microscope. Remove a plant from a balanced aquarium. With a knife or piece of glass, scrape the surface of one of the leaves and obtain a drop of water. Place this drop on a glass slide and cover it with a thin piece of glass. The microscope will show many kinds of tiny living things.

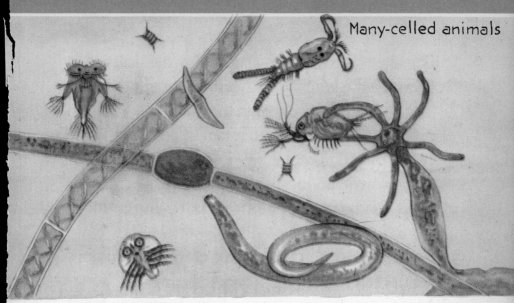

Man and His Food

Many thousands of years ago, man obtained his food wherever he could find it, just as most animals do today. During certain times of the year little food could be found, and people became very hungry. All foods had to be eaten raw, because man had not learned to use fire for cooking. Foods could not be brought from faraway places in winter because there were no trains or ships.

Unlike most animals, man is able to learn from experience. By the use of language, he is also able to tell others what he has learned.

During thousands of years, man has learned a great deal about foods. He has found many kinds of plants and animals that are good to eat. He has learned to plant seeds and grow crops for food. He has domesticated animals that provide food. He has learned to cook, to keep foods from spoiling and to bring foods from faraway places.

Like most animals, many of man's activities are centered around the securing of food. More people are engaged in growing foods than in any other occupation. Packing, canning, storing, cooking and serving foods are other important occupations. If it were not necessary to eat, most people would have little work to do.

Useful Substances in Foods

Six main kinds of useful substances are found in foods: proteins, carbohydrates, fats, vitamins, minerals and water. These substances are found in different amounts in different kinds of food.

Eggs, lean meat, peas and beans are examples of foods that contain a great deal of protein. A large part of the bodies of people and animals is composed of protein. Protein is needed for growth. It is also needed to furnish materials for the repair of parts that become worn out.

Carbohydrates include both sugars and starches. Ordinary sugar is a pure carbohydrate. Potatoes, bread and most root vegetables are foods that contain large amounts of starch. Carbohydrates do not help animals to grow. Their main use is to supply heat to keep animals warm and to give them energy for motion.

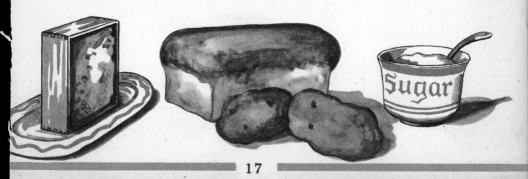

Foods that contain fats also supply heat and energy. Animals store fat in their bodies, and plants store it in nuts and seeds. Milk, meat and nuts are the main sources of fats.

Vitamins are found in foods in very small quantities. Fresh foods usually contain more vitamins than dried, canned or cooked foods. Although only small amounts of vitamins are needed, good health cannot be maintained without these chemical substances.

Animals need minerals to build the hard parts of their bodies, especially the bones and teeth. Meats and leafy vegetables are good sources of minerals.

Water is contained in all foods but not in sufficient quantities to supply the needs of most animals. Large healthy animals require plenty of water in addition to the foods they eat.

Digestion and Distribution of Foods

Every kind of animal uses food to produce heat and energy and to provide materials for growth and repair. Though all animals are interesting to study, we are most interested in man. We use food in the same way that the four-footed animals do, and our bodies are like theirs in many ways. By studying ourselves we can also learn a great deal about animals in general.

When food is eaten it passes into the alimentary canal. Here the food is digested and the useful substances are removed for use in the body. In man, this is a tube about thirty feet long, most of which lies coiled up in the abdomen. Every four-footed animal has an alimentary canal very much like that of man.

The alimentary canal begins with the mouth. The front teeth are used for cutting and the back teeth for grinding food. As food is eaten it is mixed with saliva. Saliva softens the food and makes it easier to swallow. It also contains certain chemicals which aid in digestion.

The stomach plays an important part in digestion. The food is carried to the stomach through a tube called the esophagus. When the stomach is empty, it is shaped like the letter "J". After a heavy meal, it is pear-shaped. The walls of the stomach contain strong muscles which help to mix the food while it is being digested. In the lining of the stomach are thousands of little glands which pour out chemicals. These chemicals help in digestion.

After remaining in the stomach for about three hours, the partly digested food passes into the small intestine. The small intestine is a tube about twenty feet long and an inch across. Wave-like motions in the muscle walls of the intestine push the food along as it is digested. Many glands pour chemicals into the intestine to help in digestion.

When the food reaches the end of the small intestine, digestion is usually completed. The unused part passes on into the large intestine. Wave-like motions run along the large intestine and finally expel the unused part of the food materials from the body.

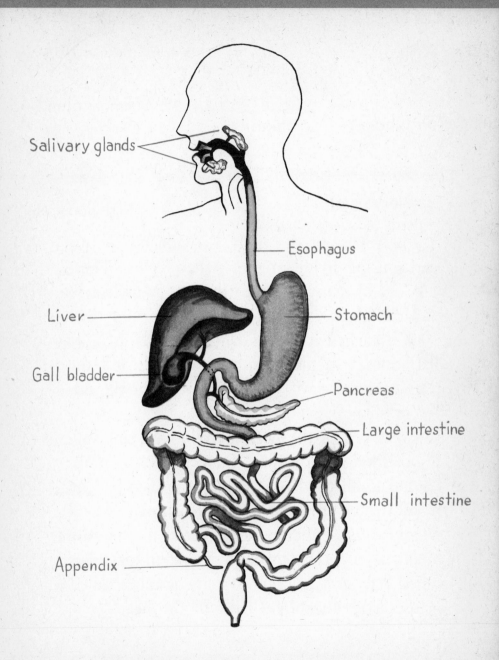

Salivary glands

Esophagus

Liver

Stomach

Gall bladder

Pancreas

Large intestine

Small intestine

Appendix

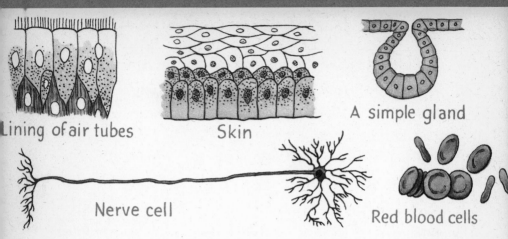

Lining of air tubes

Skin

A simple gland

Nerve cell

Red blood cells

Every part of the body is made up of tiny particles of living matter called cells. These cells are of many different shapes. Muscle cells are like fibers. Nerve cells are long and thin, with branches at the ends. Skin cells are like flat scales; red blood cells are round; and the cells of other parts of the body have still different shapes.

Every cell of the body needs a constant supply of food and oxygen. Food and oxygen are carried to all the body cells by the blood. The blood makes up about one eleventh of the total weight of the body. The heart pumps the blood to the cells through a system of tubes called arteries. Another system of tubes called veins carries the blood back to the heart.

The heart is located high in the chest, just below the neck. It is a hollow, muscular organ about the size of your fist. A partition through the center of the heart divides it into a right half and a left half. Each half of the heart is further divided into two parts, connected with valves which allow the blood to flow in only one direction. The two upper cavities of the heart are called auricles, and the two lower ones are called ventricles. When the heart beats, the muscle contracts and blood is forced out through the arteries. Between beats, blood flows back into the heart from the veins.

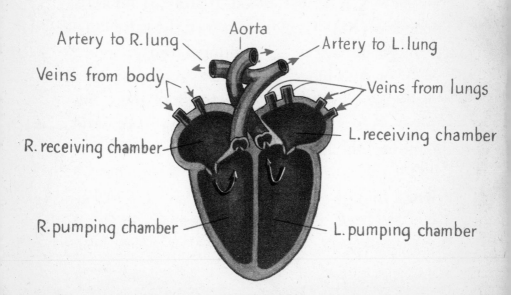

Artery to R. lung   Aorta   Artery to L. lung

Veins from body   Veins from lungs

R. receiving chamber   L. receiving chamber

R. pumping chamber   L. pumping chamber

With the help of the diagram on page 27, let us trace the course of the blood through the body and find out how food and oxygen are brought to the cells. This diagram shows some of the larger blood vessels and a few of the main organs. In studying this diagram, it is necessary to remember that, when a person faces us, his right side is at our left. That is the reason the right side of the heart in the diagram is on our left. The blood contains food materials at all times, but it must return to the lungs about every two minutes to pick up oxygen. Beginning with the right auricle (R.A.), the blood passes to the right ventricle (R.V.). It is then forced to the lungs through an artery. The lungs contain a network of fine blood tubes. Oxygen passes into the blood through the thin walls of these fine tubes. After remaining in the lungs about half a minute, the blood is carried back into the left auricle (L.A.) through a vein. From here it passes into the left ventricle (L.V.) and out into the rest of the body through a large artery called the aorta.

Only a very few of the millions of branches of the aorta are shown in the diagram. The branching is somewhat like that of a tree, and the aorta may be thought of as the trunk of the tree. Large branches run to the head, arms, legs and other main parts of the body. Smaller branches, like the twigs of trees, extend outward from the large branches. The arteries end in very fine tubes called capillaries, which connect with the small branches of veins.

Every body cell must have a constant supply of food and oxygen. Food and oxygen enter the cells by escaping from the blood through the thin walls of the capillary tubes. Capillary tubes are very numerous and close together.

The cells of the body could live for only a few minutes without oxygen. That is why we must continue to breathe in oxygen at all times, even while we are asleep. The body cells also require a constant supply of food at all times. But we do not need to eat all the time because there is usually a supply of digested food in the intestine. Large amounts of food materials are also stored in the liver.

Artery

Vein

A CAPILLARY

The heart must continue to beat at all times in order that food and oxygen may be brought to the cells by the blood. People sometimes wonder how the heart can continue beating without any rest. The answer is that the heart rests between beats. The heart beats about eighty times a minute, but there is a fraction of a second between beats during which the heart does no work. On the average, the heart really works only about nine hours each day and gets fifteen hours rest. As the heart pumps the blood through the body, most of it goes to the muscles which remove food materials from the blood. Smaller amounts go to the brain and other parts which also require food. To make up for this loss of food from the blood, there are large arteries which go to the intestine and liver where the blood picks up more food.

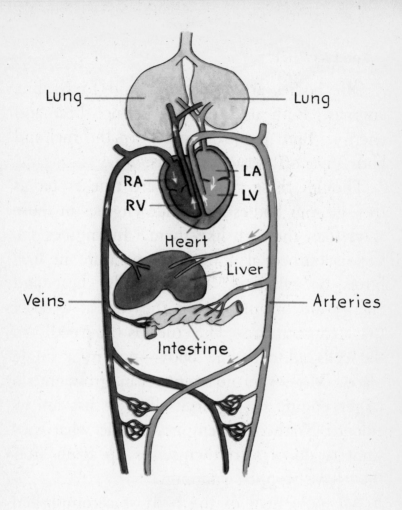

Lung — — Lung

RA — — LA
RV — — LV

Heart

— Liver

Veins — — Arteries

Intestine

Oxygen enters the blood in the lungs. Blood that is returning
from the lungs is brighter red in color than blood
that is going to the lungs

Food as Fuel

Our bodies are sometimes said to be like engines. Both use fuel to produce heat and energy. Both require air to burn the fuel and both give off waste products.

Though these statements are true as far as they go, our bodies are unlike engines in more ways than they are like them. In engines the fuel is burned at a high temperature in fire-boxes or cylinders. In the body, heat and energy are obtained from the fuel at a fairly low temperature. The fuel is "burned" in the cells all over the body—not in a single place. Moreover, no engine can grow into a larger engine or repair itself if it has an accident. Neither can engines decide what they want to do or start themselves up again after they have stopped running.

All movement of the body is accomplished by means of muscles. Muscles are composed of cells joined end to end so as to form long fibers. Bundles of these muscle fibers bound together make up the different muscles.

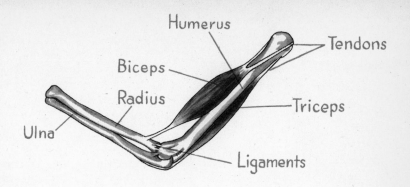

Like the other cells of the body, the muscle
cells are fitted to do a single kind of work.
The only thing that muscle cells can do is to
contract. In doing this they become shorter
and thicker. When the millions of muscle
cells within a muscle all contract at the same
time, the whole muscle becomes shorter.

The diagram on this page shows the two
largest muscles and the bones of the arm. The
muscles are connected with the bones by strong
cords called tendons. There are soft pads at
the ends of the bones with an oily liquid between them. This allows the bones to be
moved easily and freely. The ends of the
bones are tied to each other by cords called
ligaments.

The big muscle that we feel above the elbow when we bend the arm is the biceps muscle. The muscle at the back of the arm is the triceps. When the biceps muscle contracts, the tendons pull on the bones in such a way that the arm is bent. When we wish to straighten out the arm, the triceps muscle must contract. As the arm is straightened, the biceps muscle is stretched out again.

The muscles of the fingers, toes, legs, back, neck and other parts of the body are also arranged in pairs. When one muscle moves a body part in a certain direction, another muscle must pull it back again. Most movements of the body require the use of more than one pair of muscles. In such exercises as swimming,

running and playing ping-pong, nearly all the large muscles are put to use.

During vigorous exercise, the muscle cells require more food and oxygen than when they are at rest. The heart pumps faster to supply this food and oxygen. As food materials unite with the oxygen in the cells, a great deal of heat energy is released. The body then feels warmer than usual. On a cold day or at times when we are taking no exercise, the body often feels cooler than usual. But whether we feel warm or cold, the blood is kept at a temperature between 98 degrees F. and 99 degrees F. at all times, except during severe illness.

The temperature of the blood is kept constant in several ways. During vigorous exercise, more blood flows into the skin than at other times. Heat can thus escape from the body. While we are at rest on a cold day, very little blood flows through the skin, and the heat is retained within the body. When the body becomes very warm, we perspire. Evaporation of water from the moist skin is very cooling. A great deal of heat also leaves the body in the warm air that is exhaled from the lungs.

Cells and Growth

When a snowball is rolled through soft snow, it becomes larger and larger. Likewise,

when a crystal of sugar is fastened to a string and the string is lowered into a thick sugar solution, the crystal becomes larger and larger. Both the snowball and the sugar crystal seem to grow, but this kind of growth is due to the addition of more material to the outside of an object. The body does not grow in the same way that snowballs and sugar crystals do. It grows by adding material from the inside.

When we eat pea soup, pork chops, cheese or hamburger sandwiches, the food materials must first be digested so that they will be able to pass through the walls of the intestine. They must then be carried by the blood to the cells.

CELL DIVISION

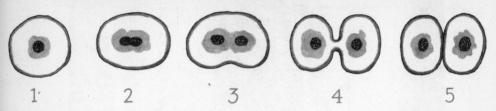

1   2   3   4   5

A boy twelve years old weighs several times as much as he did when he was born. Part of this growth is due to the addition of more cells to his body. Cells are added to the body by the dividing of old cells. When a cell divides, each of the two new cells is only half as large as the cell from which it came. But these half-sized cells soon become full-sized cells by adding substances contained in foods.

A second way in which the body grows is by the enlargement of cells already present. Most parts of the body do not add new cells after birth. A muscle that has plenty of exercise grows larger because the cells become larger, not because new cells are added. Nerve cells in the arms and legs become longer as the body grows taller. In the growth of cells, the principal food substances that are used are proteins.

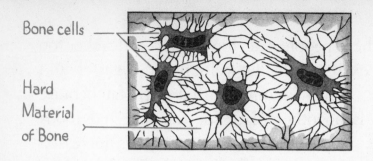

Bone cells

Hard
Material
of Bone

There is still a third way in which growth takes place. Some kinds of cells remove substances from the blood and deposit them as hard materials. Bone cells, for example, deposit mineral matter around themselves. The teeth grow in a similar way. In order to form strong bones and teeth, minerals must be present in the food. Leafy vegetables, milk, eggs and meat contain minerals.

Under the skin and between the muscles are large numbers of fat cells. These cells are like little pockets; they store food by filling themselves with fat. They give the body a rounded and pleasing appearance.

FAT CELLS

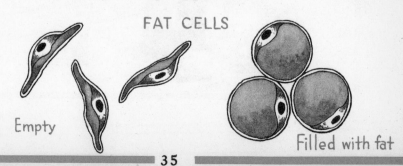

Empty

Filled with fat

When people eat too much and take too little exercise, the fat cells become larger and larger. They become stuffed with fat because there is no other place for the digested foods to go. If the amount of exercise is increased and the amount of food is decreased, the fat cells are forced to give up some of their fat. The body then becomes slimmer again.

Things to Do

1. Watch different animals eat and drink.
2. Make a list of animals and the foods they eat.
3. Place some hay in a bottle and fill the bottle with water. After two or three weeks, remove a drop from the surface of the water and look at it under a microscope. It should contain some tiny animals.
4. Place a little corn starch in a test tube or small bottle. Add water and mix thoroughly. Now add a drop or two of iodine.
5. Test foods for starch by adding iodine.
6. Learn to take your pulse rate.
7. Make a model of an arm, similar to the one shown below.

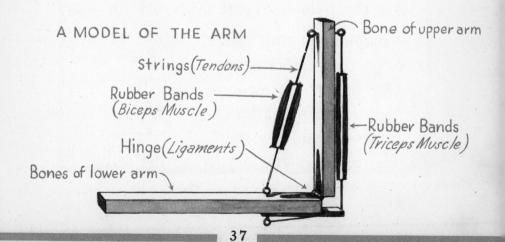

A MODEL OF THE ARM

Bone of upper arm

Strings (*Tendons*)

Rubber Bands (*Biceps Muscle*)

Hinge (*Ligaments*)

Bones of lower arm

←Rubber Bands (*Triceps Muscle*)

Name several foods that are good sources of each of the following:

Proteins *Eggs, lean meat, peas, beans*
Fats *Milk, meat, nuts*
Carbohydrates *spuds, bread, sugar, most vegetables*
Minerals *Meats, leafy vegetables*
Vitamins *Fresh foods*
Water *is contained in almost all foods*

Match each animal's name with a food that the animal eats:

bat — *mosquitoes*   ants
flicker — *ants*   clams
gull — *clams*   fish
horse — *grass*   grass
raccoon — *fish*   mosquitoes

Are the following statements true or false?

1. Vitamins are tiny plants. *false*
2. Sugar is a carbohydrate. *true*
3. Our fingers are made up of cells. *true*
4. Veins are small arteries. *false*
5. Bones contain minerals. *true*
6. The blood carries oxygen to the cells. *true*

Copy and Fill in the Blanks

1. Oxygen enters the blood in the *lungs*.
2. The upper cavities of the heart are called *right and left ventricle*.
3. The tube that connects the mouth with the stomach is called the *esophagus*.
4. Tubes that carry blood away from the heart are called *arteries*.
5. The average temperature of the body is about *98–99° F.*
6. The muscles are connected with the bones by strong cords called *tendrons*.

Topics for Further Study

1. Appendix
2. Brain
3. Breathing
4. Crystals
5. Flickers
6. Glands
7. Gulls
8. Liver
9. Lungs
10. Lymph
11. Mosquitoes
12. Mountain goats
13. Oysters
14. Porcupines
15. Red blood cells
16. Rotifers
17. Spiders
18. Teeth
19. Vitamins
20. White blood cells

Questions

1. What is the chief problem of animals?
2. How do different grazing animals eat grass?
3. How do sea gulls open clam shells?
4. How do clams eat?
5. How does an ameba eat?
6. In what different ways are foods useful to animals?
7. What are the parts of the alimentary canal?
8. Why is digestion necessary?
9. Which glands help in digestion? How?
10. What are cells?
11. How do the cells of the body get food and oxygen?
12. How is the body like an engine?
13. How is the body unlike an engine?
14. Why is it important that we eat foods which contain minerals and vitamins?
15. How do muscles move the body?
16. How does the body grow?
17. How is the temperature of the body kept about the same at all times?

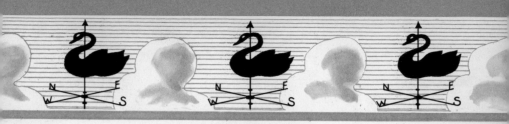

WEATHER AND CLIMATE

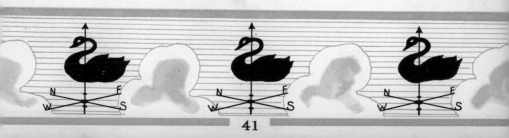

Measuring Air Changes

What will the weather be tomorrow? The answer to this question is important to farmers, fishermen, aviators and workers in many other occupations. In former times, people tried to predict the weather by watching the flights of birds, the movements of clouds, the colors of sunsets and by other signs. Today more scientific means are used to predict tomorrow's weather.

The main office of the United States Weather Bureau is in Washington, D. C. About three hundred branch stations are maintained in various parts of the country. These stations make several reports daily to the main station and to each other. In addition, daily reports of weather conditions are received from about one hundred Canadian stations, from Alaska, the West Indies and from ships at sea. From sounding balloons miles above the earth come radio signals that report air conditions in the upper atmosphere. The data gathered from these sources form the basis of the weather predictions which are broadcast over the radio and published in newspapers.

When we say that the weather is warm, what we really mean is that the air is warm. When we say it is windy, we mean that the air is in motion. Without changes in the air, we would have no change in weather at all. Every day would be just like every other day; there would be no summer, no winter, no wind, no rain and no clouds.

Scientists are interested in measuring things. Weather scientists, called meteorologists, try to measure air conditions. When they find out what changes in air conditions are taking place and how rapidly they are taking place, they are usually able to tell almost exactly what tomorrow's weather will be. In order to measure air conditions accurately, certain instruments are necessary.

The instrument used to measure the temperature of the air is, of course, the thermometer. The liquid in the bulb of a thermometer expands when it is heated by the surrounding air. This causes the liquid to rise in the thermometer tube. When the air around the bulb of a thermometer becomes cooler, the liquid cools and contracts and drops lower in the tube. Marks on the side of the tube show the exact temperature of the air.

Thermometer

A very sensitive kind of thermometer can be made by inserting a piece of glass tubing into a bottle fitted with a one-hole stopper. Fasten the bottle in an inverted position over a jar of colored water so that the end of the tubing is under water. Now warm the outside of the bottle with your hands to force out a little of the air. When the air inside the bottle becomes the same temperature as the outside air, the colored water will rise in the tube. Even slight changes in temperature will cause the colored water to rise and fall in the tube.

The pressure of the air is measured by an instrument called a barometer. Fit a rubber stopper connected with a tube into the opening of a large tin can, and draw out some of the air. The air pressure on the outside of the can will cause the sides to bulge inward. The

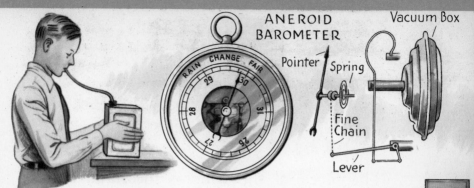

ANEROID
BAROMETER

Vacuum Box

Pointer Spring

Fine
Chain

Lever

RAIN CHANGE FAIR
29 30
28 31
27 26

pressure of the air can be found by means of an instrument that uses the same principle. The side of a small metal box, from which most of the air has been removed, is connected with a pointer that moves along a dial. When the air pressure increases, the pointer moves in one direction. When the air pressure decreases, the pointer moves in the opposite direction. In another kind of barometer, changes in air pressure cause mercury to rise and fall in a glass tube.

Many different kinds of instruments are used to find the amount of moisture in the air. One of the most interesting is an instrument made of a single human hair which is attached to a lever that moves a pointer. The hair lengthens and shortens as the amount of moisture in the air changes.

Mercury
Barometer

32
31
30
29
28

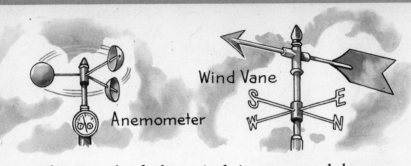

Wind Vane

Anemometer

The speed of the wind is measured by an instrument called an anemometer. Cup-shaped vessels are fastened to arms which revolve when the wind blows. The faster the wind blows, the faster they revolve. The turning shaft is attached to a speedometer. The pointer of this speedometer indicates the speed of the wind in miles per hour.

Wind vanes show the wind direction. These are often seen on the tops of buildings and are very simple to make and understand. Air socks are used at flying fields because they are large enough to be seen from a great distance.

In order to predict the weather accurately, conditions in the upper air as well as conditions near the ground must be known. Sounding balloons now used by the Weather Bureau for this purpose are ordinary rubber balloons that are inflated with either hydrogen or helium.

Attached to each balloon is a parachute with a small box containing weather instruments and a radio broadcasting set. The balloons are inflated with gas until they are about five feet in diameter. When released, they ascend at a speed of about six hundred feet per minute. As the balloons rise, signals from the broadcasting sets are picked up automatically at the ground station.

Because of the decrease in air pressure, a sounding balloon expands as it rises. At a height of about fifteen miles above the earth, it expands to a diameter of about fifteen feet and bursts. The instruments keep broadcasting the temperature, pressure and moisture content of the air as they come down in the parachute.

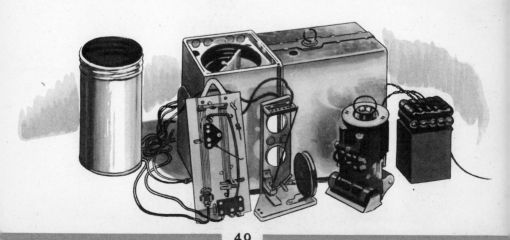

The direction and speed of the wind at various levels of the atmosphere are discovered by following the course of a balloon with a small telescope. It often happens that a balloon will float away in one direction and be blown back in the opposite direction when it reaches a higher altitude. More than one third of the parachutes and boxes of instruments are recovered and can be used over again. The others are blown out to sea or come down in places where no one happens to find them.

The information obtained from sounding balloons and from the many weather stations on the ground, gives a fairly complete picture of the air conditions over most of North America. This information is sent out by teletype to the main weather stations located in the larger cities, to be used as the basis for predicting tomorrow's weather.

Forecasting without Instruments

A favorite story among workers in the Weather Bureau is the one about a well-known meteorologist who always came to work early in the morning to make the daily weather forecast. He checked his instruments carefully, assembled his reports from other stations and made up the weather map. When he was ready to leave, he always went to the window to look at the sky. He wanted to know if he would need his umbrella and overshoes.

Although this story is not quite fair to meteorologists, since about nine out of every ten of their predictions really are correct, it does show that the sky has some important

things to tell us. The appearance of the clouds, for instance, gives us several hours advance notice of changes in the weather.

There are four main types of clouds which are easy for anyone to learn and remember. Big banks of thick, dark clouds with ragged edges are called nimbus clouds. When there are nimbus clouds in the sky, rain or snow is about to fall or is already falling. The large, fluffy, cotton-like masses that appear during fair weather are called cumulus clouds.

Cirrus clouds are the thin wispy "mare's-tails" that float across the sky at great altitudes. Sometimes these clouds rise as high as the lower level of the stratosphere. Cirrus clouds are composed of ice crystals and may travel at a speed as great as 200 miles per hour.

Stratus clouds, as their name indicates, are in layers. Sometimes the layers may be partly broken up by the wind. At other times the layers thicken into unbroken, gray masses.

The important thing to know about the different kinds of clouds is that they almost always follow each other in a definite order.

CIRRUS

The first clouds to appear after a period of fair weather are the cirrus clouds. If they are thin and the sky is blue, there will usually be fair weather for at least twenty-four hours. If they form a thick blanket, rain or snow is near.

After the cirrus clouds, come the stratus clouds. Gray stratus clouds are almost a sure sign of rain or snow. Unless the wind changes, they thicken and form nimbus or rain clouds. When the rain is over, the nimbus clouds break up and the sky becomes clear again. Cumulus clouds then soon appear in the sky.

CUMULUS

STRATUS

No matter whether you understand how a barometer works or not, or whether you know the difference between an isobar and an iceberg, a knowledge of the parade of clouds will give you a good start in learning to predict the weather.

Cirrus, stratus, nimbus, cumulus is the usual order, but there are some exceptions. If, however, you keep a record of the daily weather, including the temperature, the direction of the wind and the rainfall, you will soon learn how to allow for the exceptions.

NIMBUS

Observations of the forms of clouds give us much the same kind of information about air conditions that meteorologists get when they read a barometer. Clouds can also serve as a weather vane to indicate the direction of the wind. For this purpose observe only those clouds that are directly overhead, as you may be badly fooled by clouds near the horizon. If the clouds are moving slowly, support your head against some object in order to make sure that it is the clouds that are moving and not your head.

The speed of the wind may be estimated by watching trees and waves. When leaves barely move, the wind speed is between two and five miles per hour. When twigs and branches sway, the wind speed is between six and fifteen miles per hour. A wind of from twenty-six to forty miles per hour will raise white caps on lakes and sway the tops of trees. A wind

speed of from forty to sixty miles per hour is called a gale, and one of from sixty to eighty miles per hour is a hurricane.

Even the temperature can be determined quite accurately without instruments. It has been found that the higher the temperature, the faster ants travel. Crickets also make good thermometers. Count the chirps that a cricket makes in fourteen seconds, add forty and the total will be the Fahrenheit temperature.

Do not expect to become an expert weather forecaster in a week. Long observation is required to learn the signs that foretell weather changes. Though it may seem at first that the weather is fickle and has many tricks, it really acts according to strict scientific laws. When the forecaster knows enough about weather laws, he can forecast the weather. Sometimes a forecaster is wrong, but the weather never is.

One of the first things that a successful weather forecaster must learn is to beware of weather superstitions. Most of the signs connected with the sun, moon and stars are false and have nothing to do with the weather. Many people, when they see certain streaks in the sky, say that the sun is "drawing water." This is a very silly belief because it is well known that the sun is millions of miles away. The moon does not "hold water" either, so it makes no difference how it is tipped.

Weather forecasters should beware of forecasting the weather too far ahead. Some people will tell you that when geese fly south earlier than usual, it will be a cold winter. What really happens is that food is scarce, and the geese are off in search of a place where food is plentiful. The same people are likely to believe that when animals know a very cold winter is coming, they grow a thicker coat of fur than usual. What really happens is that during good seasons, animals get plenty of food and are able to grow better fur than usual. It would be difficult to predict the weather from such facts as these.

Air Masses and Precipitation

Much of our weather comes to us from far-away places. Great masses of warm air collect over the desert regions of the southwestern part of our country. Great masses of moist air collect over oceans and lakes. Great masses of cold air collect in the polar regions. These masses of air move and shift about because of the earth's rotation on its axis, because of the location of continents and oceans on the earth's surface and because of the difference in temperature between the poles and the equator. One of the chief jobs of the Weather Bureau is to keep track of the movements of air masses.

The temperature, pressure and amount of moisture within a large air mass tend to remain about the same. If a mass of warm air moves northward, it brings warm weather. If a mass of cold air moves southward, it brings cold weather. This is one reason for the heat waves of summer and the cold waves of winter.

The dividing line between two masses of air is called a front. When a mass of warm air

meets a mass of cold air, the cold air flows under the warm air because it is heavier. This pushes the warm air upward and clouds form all along the front. As the warm air continues to rise, it becomes cooler, and moisture condenses as rain or snow.

Within the large air masses, smaller air masses push each other about from day to day and sometimes from hour to hour. Cool air is heavier than warm air. Over the hot streets of a city, there is often a rising current of warm air, while cooler air flows in to take its place. As the warm air rises, it cools. There may then be a local shower, because cool air cannot hold as much moisture as warm air can.

On a calm day in summer, a layer of warm air often collects over the hot ground. Above it is a layer of cooler, heavier air. As the sun continues to shine, the layer of warm air becomes thicker and takes up more moisture. In this way it becomes so much lighter than the layer of air above that something has to happen. What usually happens is that the mass of warm air presses upward on the layer of cool air, and finally breaks through. As the warm air rushes through the opening in the layer of cool air, the moisture begins to condense and form big dark clouds. The clouds rise so rapidly that raindrops form and there is a sudden shower. The water particles become charged with electricity because of the rapid air movements. Lightning flashes between the

ground and the clouds. Thunder rumbles in echoes among the clouds.

A cloud can be formed in a gallon jug in the following way. Place a few drops of gasoline in the jug. The purpose of the gasoline is to provide particles on which the moisture of the air can condense. (The raindrops from real clouds condense on dust particles in the air, but there will not be enough of these in a gallon of air to form a thick cloud.) Connect a pump and force as much air into the jug as possible. This will increase the air pressure. Now release the pressure by disconnecting the pump. The pressure will be reduced in much the same way as it is reduced in a rising current of air. A thick cloud should form in the jug.

Rain, mist, hail, sleet and snow are all forms of precipitation. Water that falls in these different forms is collected and measured in rain gauges. The Weather Bureau keeps records of the amount of precipitation for all parts of the United States. In some places the annual precipitation is about two inches, and in others it is over one hundred inches.

Hail usually forms in high clouds. Water first condenses and freezes as raindrops. The frozen drops grow larger as more moisture condenses. As they fall, they are lifted upward by rising air currents, and another layer of ice forms around them. Sometimes hailstones as large as baseballs, with as many as twenty-five layers, are formed in this way. Sleet is frozen single raindrops. Snow is frozen water vapor. Dew, fog and frost also are formed from the moisture of the air, but the Weather Bureau does not regard them as forms of precipitation.

Stormy Weather

Every aviator knows that it is easier to fly eastward than westward. An airplane trip from New York to Los Angeles usually takes several hours longer than one from Los Angeles to New York, and requires about 15 per cent more gasoline. The reason is that the winds generally blow across the United States in an easterly direction.

Of course, the wind does not always blow directly eastward. Often it moves in great whirlpools that the weather man calls "highs" and "lows." These great whirling masses of air move across the country at a speed of about five hundred miles per day in summer and about seven hundred miles per day in winter.

A "high" means an area of high air pressure. A quantity of cool, dry air is heavier than an equal quantity of warm, moist air. Within a high, the heavy air moves downward toward the earth and then spreads out from a center. "Highs" are areas of fair weather.

"Lows" are areas of rainy or stormy weather. At the center of a low there is an upward current of air, and the surrounding air moves inward. Since the inward moving air does not blow directly toward the center, the whole mass of air in the low is given a whirling motion and is called a cyclone. Cyclones are often 1000 miles in diameter. The southeast quarter of a cyclone is usually the stormiest.

When the air over a desert or large plain becomes heated to a high temperature, air currents rise very rapidly. This may cause a whirlwind, or tornado. A funnel-shaped cloud results, in which the air spins around at a speed of as much as 500 miles per hour. Animals, trees and buildings sometimes are caught in whirlwinds and carried several miles away.

Whirlwinds are the cause of the most violent storms at sea. In the Atlantic Ocean these disturbances are called hurricanes, and in the Pacific Ocean they are called typhoons. Some of the most destructive of these storms come out of

the Caribbean Sea, and occasionally one swings up the coast of the United States.

The worst hurricane on record took place on September 21, 1938. It traveled through the Atlantic Ocean in a great curved path and struck the coast of Long Island and New England. The Weather Bureau sent out warnings, and fishing boats scurried for shelter. When the storm moved in from the ocean, the water rose twenty feet and washed away many houses from the beaches. A wind of at least 200 miles per hour mowed down trees and snapped off church steeples. Roofs were torn from houses, and boats anchored in harbors were tossed up on the land!

Floods as well as winds can cause tremendous damage. The flood in the spring of 1927 was the worst in the history of our country. Unusually heavy rains during the fall and winter had soaked the ground. Thousands of small streams and rivers were filled to overflowing. Then came the melting of the winter snows and the warm spring rains. As the soil became warmer, it released much of its stored water. The water from twenty-one states rushed down the Mississippi River toward the sea.

Of course all this water could not pour out of the mouth of the Mississippi at once. The water rose higher and higher. Finally the river overflowed its banks and flooded a strip of land 1000 miles long and 50 miles wide.

Two long months passed before the water lowered to its normal level. The valley was in ruin. Hundreds had lost their lives. Others lost crops, livestock, homes and property. There was constant suffering because of the lack of safe drinking water and the scarcity of food. The people of the Mississippi Valley cannot forget the flood, or cease to fear the great river.

Every time a great deal of snow falls in and around New York, the older people are reminded of the great Blizzard of 1888. The newspapers published pictures and stories of what happened on March 12 of that year. In six hours the heavy snowfall wrapped the great city in a blanket of white, and shut it away from the rest of the world. Electric wires went down, and the city was in darkness. Elevated trains stopped, and the passengers gladly paid fifty cents each to be helped down on ladders. Street cars did not run for four days. Train service was discontinued. Telephone and telegraph services were out of order. Drifts reached second- and third-story windows. It was impossible to get food delivered, and most difficult to go after it. New Yorkers had weather worth talking about for many years to come.

Great snowstorms often occur in other parts of the country. In Minnesota, for example, the snow now and then gets so deep that farmers can drive their sleds over the tops of the fences. In places where snow has drifted, people have been known to walk on the snow to a telephone pole, and to sit down on the crossarm.

Sometimes a small amount of water can cause a great deal of trouble. Fog is really a low cloud which contains only a few quarts more water per cubic mile than clear air does. Yet it is fog that makes aviation and navigation so dangerous. A few quarts of water in the form of fog once tied up the harbor of New York for forty hours. During that time eight ocean liners collided, and twenty or more ships could not dock.

When a great number of dust particles are carried by the wind at a high rate of speed, we have what is known as a dust or sand storm. Dust particles spreading over Europe in the year 1773 formed such a heavy veil or haze that some people feared the end of the world was at hand. Later they learned that the "Great Haze" was caused by tiny particles of rock that had drifted from a volcano in Iceland. The "Blood Rains," which formerly aroused so much excitement in Europe, were caused by the tiny bits of reddish dust blown northward from the Sahara Desert. The dust was washed down by the rain which had a reddish color as it fell. In our own country during 1934, great clouds of dust were blown from the prairie states all the way to the Atlantic Ocean.

Nowadays, people wonder what has become of Indian Summer. In former times there were several weeks of hazy autumn weather, caused by the smoke blown from the fires in prairie grass and forests. Now that there is no prairie grass to burn and forest fires are better controlled, we miss much of our autumn haze.

Indoors, man has been able to create almost ideal weather, but he has not succeeded in doing much about the outdoor weather. He has tried shooting cannon to stop hailstorms, but without success. Mysterious devices have been set up by people who claimed to be able to make it rain. Sometimes it did rain, but probably it would have anyway. Small showers have been produced by sending airplanes to sprinkle dust on clouds. But, in spite of these efforts, we must take the weather as it comes.

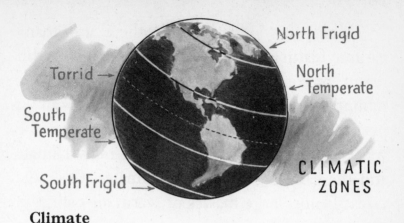

North Frigid

Torrid →

North
← Temperate

South
Temperate →

South Frigid →

CLIMATIC
ZONES

Climate

The average of the weather conditions of a certain place over a period of time is known as climate. Both the Northern and Southern hemispheres are divided, for convenience of study, into three climatic zones. The Torrid Zone, which lies nearest the equator, has an even climate with rather high temperatures every month of the year. In the Temperate Zones the climate is more changeable, though the South Temperate Zone, because of its large ocean surfaces, has a more even temperature than the North Temperate Zone. In the Frigid Zones, the temperature ranges in some places from 90 degrees Fahrenheit above zero in summer to over 90 degrees below in winter.

Within the United States there are many natural features that affect the climate of different regions. As the winds blow over the mountains along the West Coast, the air is pushed upward and cooled. This gives the western slopes of the mountains a rainy climate and the eastern slopes a dry climate. Over the Great Plains, large masses of warm air collect in summer, and large masses of cold air collect in winter. This causes extremes in temperature almost as great as those that occur in the Frigid Zones. Around the Great Lakes and along the Atlantic Ocean and Gulf of Mexico, the temperature is more even because of the nearness to large bodies of water.

Evidence of recent climatic changes is shown by the difference in the growth rings of the big trees of California. In favorable years, trees grow well and form wider wood rings than they do in unfavorable years. By studying the growth rings of hundreds of trees, some of which were more than three thousand years old, scientists have been able to trace the changes in climate over long periods of time.

According to the trees, there was a period of dry weather from 1400 B.C. until 1240 B.C., and a period of favorable climate which lasted until 660 B.C. Dry periods then alternated with favorable climate until 880 A.D., when another period of wet weather began. From 1100 A.D. until 1200 A.D. it was dry again. The last great stormy period lasted from 1300 to 1400 A.D.

Glaciers have left evidence of the climate of still more ancient times. At least four times, enormous glaciers have crept down from the north, cutting great grooves in the earth. When the glaciers melted, they left giant boulders on the ground. Between these periods of glaciers there were periods of very warm weather all over the earth. Tropical vegetation grew near the poles and left large coal deposits.

Several theories have been suggested to explain the past changes in the earth's climate. One theory is that huge dust clouds from outer space may have drifted into the solar system and shut out a part of the sun's light. Dust from volcanoes may have had a similar effect, since it is known that cooler weather followed the explosion of a volcano in Alaska in 1912. Dust from such explosions enters the stratosphere and may be carried around the earth several times.

Another interesting theory is that the greater the amount of land area on the earth, the colder the climate becomes. At the time that the dinosaurs lived, the land was low and swampy. Oceans were shallow and covered almost the entire earth. This made the climate warm. Later, when the present continents were formed, the climate became cold. A small change in the earth's average temperature would, even now, change the climate suddenly. It has been estimated that with a drop of even four degrees all over the earth, glaciers would form again, bringing on another ice age.

Things to Do

1. Make a table with spaces for recording temperature, wind direction, wind speed, kinds of clouds and amount of rain or snow. Keep a daily record of the weather.
2. Make a wind vane or air sock and place it where it can be seen from the window.
3. Make a rain gauge.
4. Report on how different plants and animals protect themselves against bad weather.
5. Make a thermometer from a bottle, a piece of glass tubing, a rubber stopper and colored water. Make a scale for it with the aid of another thermometer.
6. Collect pictures showing the effects of storms, hurricanes, tornadoes and other unusual weather conditions.
7. Study weather maps, rainfall maps and maps showing wind belts and ocean currents.
8. Report on the work of the U. S. Weather Bureau.
9. Make a list of weather superstitions.

Tell the Correct Answers

1. Thermometers are used to measure
   <u>temperature</u> air pressure wind direction

2. Anemometers are used to measure
   wind direction <u>wind speed</u> air pressure

3. Barometers are used to measure
   temperature <u>air pressure</u> wind speed

4. Wind vanes are used to measure
   air pressure <u>wind direction</u> wind speed

5. Stratus clouds always appear
   white black <u>in layers</u>

6. Cirrus clouds are composed of
   raindrops ice crystals <u>dust</u>

7. A wind of fifty miles per hour is a
   <u>gale</u> cyclone hurricane

8. Frozen raindrops are called
   <u>hail</u> snow sleet

9. Storm clouds are called
   nimbus clouds cirrus clouds <u>stratus clouds</u>

10. Fair weather clouds are called
    cirrus clouds <u>cumulus clouds</u> nimbus clouds

Topics for Further Study

1. Antarctica
2. Beacons
3. Coast guard
4. Foghorns
5. Greenland Ice Cap
6. Icebergs
7. Ice storms
8. Lighthouses
9. Monsoons
10. Radio sondes
11. Rime
12. Sargasso Sea
13. Snow plows
14. Storm warnings
15. Stormy petrels
16. Superstitions
17. Teletype
18. Trade winds
19. Tropical storms
20. Typhoons

Copy, and Fill in the Blanks

1. Weather scientists are called *meteorologists*
2. A wind speed of from 60 to 80 miles per hour is called a *hurricane* .
3. Rain, hail and snow are forms of *rain*.
4. "Blood rains" are caused by . . . .
5. The average weather of a place is called . . . .
6. Whirlwinds in the Pacific Ocean are called . . . .
7. When air is heated, it . . . .
8. When air is cooled, it . . . .

Questions

1. How does the Weather Bureau help farmers, fishermen and aviators?
2. What are air masses?
3. Why is it easier to fly eastward than westward across the Atlantic Ocean?
4. How does hail form?
5. What are cyclones?
6. Explain how a thermometer works.
7. Explain how an anemometer works.
8. What are "highs" and "lows"?
9. What is the cause of local showers?
10. What are superstitions?
11. What is a theory?
12. How may crickets be used to find the air temperature?
13. What instruments are used to measure the different weather conditions?
14. Name the climate zones.
15. How do we know that changes in the earth's climate have taken place in the past?
16. What theories have been advanced to explain changes in climate?

ELECTRICITY AND ITS USES

Electromagnets

Bill had been busy for a long time at his work table in the cellar. Every afternoon, when he came home from school, he seemed to have something very important to do. He was secretly making something that would surprise his friends when they came to visit him. At last, he completed the apparatus he was making. He tried it and it worked. He tried it again and again. It worked every time.

A few days later, Bill's friends surprised him with a birthday party. Of course, Bill's mother had known about the surprise party days before, and so there were plenty of good things to eat.

After the ice cream was served, Bill had an idea. This was just the time! He would show his new invention to all his friends.

"By the way," said Bill, trying not to appear excited, "I have a new gadget in the cellar that you might like to see. Just a little thing I made the other day."

Bill's friends were interested immediately and they all went down to the basement.

"Oh, isn't that lovely!" exclaimed Nancy, as she rushed over to the little fern garden in the cellar window. "That is a good idea. I'm going to make one just like it in our cellar window."

"That isn't it," answered Bill. "Over in this corner. This is what I wanted you to see."

Near Bill's work table was a long stick, supported in the middle so as to make a balance. From one end of the stick hung a small weight. A large tin can hung from the other end of the stick. Under the tin can, but not touching it, there was a big box. The box rested on a small rug. The children came closer so as to get a good look at Bill's invention.

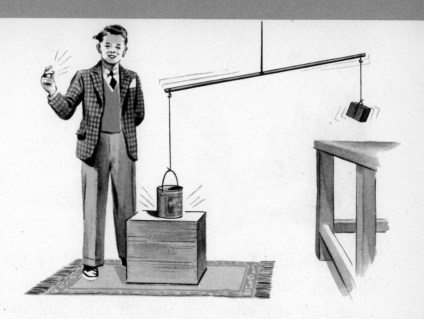

"Now," said Bill, "when I snap my fingers watch the tin can."

As he did so, the can dipped down toward the box and stayed there. The weight on the other end of the stick swung upward. Then he whistled, and the can went up, while the weight swung downward again.

"Do it again," cried several of the children.

Bill snapped his fingers, and the can dipped downward just as it had done before. He whistled, and the can moved upward again.

"Would someone else like to try my invention?" asked Bill.

"I would! I would!" cried several of the children, but no amount of snapping and whistling had any effect on the tin can. Bill did his trick once more. They watched him, but could not understand how the trick was done. Finally, they asked for an explanation.

"Well," said Bill, "suppose we look in the box under the can."

Two of the boys flipped back the rug. They saw two wires connected with a push button at the spot where Bill's foot had been.

When the box was lifted, everybody saw a large spool of wire connected with several dry cells. They also saw two wires which ran under the rug to the place where Bill had stood when he snapped his fingers.

"I see now," cried Nancy. "Snapping your fingers had nothing to do with the effects we saw. You pushed the button with your foot and made an electric connection. When you whistled, you took your foot off the button. That stopped the electricity in the spool of wire."

"That's it," laughed Bill, "but why should electricity in a spool of wire pull down the can?"

"It must be that the spool of wire becomes a magnet," said Mary. "It certainly acts like one."

"Yes," said Bill, "you are right. It's an electromagnet. I made it out of a piece of iron and a roll of bell wire."

All the boys and girls then examined the wiring, the electromagnet, the dry cells and the push button. Some of them decided to set up the same experiment in their own homes.

An electromagnet is really easy to make. Anyone can make a very good one from some insulated bell wire and an iron nail about two or three inches long. Wind the wire around the nail, leaving about four inches of wire free at each end. Try picking up some iron carpet tacks with the nail. Does winding wire around the nail make it a magnet?

If it is not yet a magnet, you must obtain a dry cell. Connect this cell with the wire coil around the nail and with a push button. The picture on this page shows exactly how to do this. Now bring the nail near some carpet tacks or other small objects made of iron and push the button. Does the nail become a magnet? Release the button. What happens?

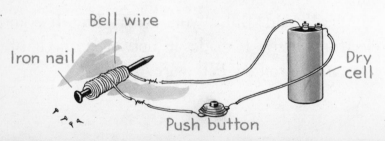

Bell wire

Iron nail

Dry cell

Push button

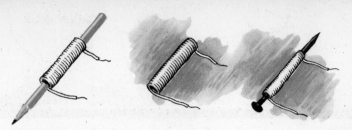

In making the electromagnet for his experiment, Bill used a large spool of wire and several dry cells, because he wanted a strong electromagnet. It had to be strong to pull down the can. Let us see how magnets of this kind can be made stronger or weaker.

Wind several electromagnets. Make one of them by winding wire around a pencil. Make another by winding wire around a pencil and then removing the pencil. Make still another by winding wire around an iron nail. Be sure that all three electromagnets have the same number of turns of wire. About twenty turns in each coil will be enough. Now connect each coil with a single dry cell. Which electromagnet will pick up the greatest number of carpet tacks? Count the number in each case.

Connect each electromagnet with two dry cells. Do the magnets become stronger when more electricity flows through the coil? How

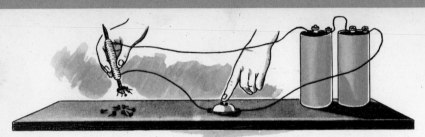

many carpet tacks does the nail electromagnet pick up when it is connected with two dry cells? From experiments of this kind we find that the greater the flow of electricity in an electromagnet, the stronger it becomes.

There is another way of making electro-magnets stronger. Wind twenty turns of a long piece of wire on an iron nail. See how many carpet tacks are held by this electromagnet. Now wind twenty more turns of the wire around the nail, making 40 turns. Again, count the number of tacks held to this electromag-net. From experiments of this kind, we find that the strength of an electromagnet can be increased by adding more turns of wire.

Once a boy wanted to make a very strong electromagnet. He had only two dry cells, but in the cellar of his house he found a huge spool of bare copper wire. He decided to wind all of it around a large iron nail. It took him half an hour to wind the coil. When it was finished, he connected it with the two dry cells. As he did so, there was a spark at the binding post. To his great surprise, the iron nail did not become a magnet at all. It could not lift a single carpet tack.

Perhaps you can guess the reason for the failure. The wire used in the coil was bare wire. Each turn touched the one next to it. Each layer of wire touched the layer above and the layer beneath. The iron nail was enclosed in bare copper wire instead of in an insulated coil. The electric current flowed straight through the copper instead of through the wire around and around the iron nail. The nail did not become a magnet, because an electromagnet can be made only with a wire coil in which the copper turns do not touch. That is why insulated wire must be used rather than bare wire.

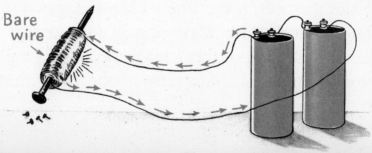

Bare wire

Very strong electromagnets can be made by wrapping the coil of wire around a long piece of iron shaped like a horseshoe. The picture on this page shows how to wind a horseshoe electromagnet. Notice that there is very little wire on the bend of the horseshoe. Nearly all of the wire is at the ends or poles of the magnet. Such an electromagnet is stronger, because both poles work together.

In factories where steel is manufactured, strong electromagnets are often used to raise and lower heavy pieces of iron. Such electromagnets are also used to load scrap iron which is hard to handle by other means. The electromagnets are attached to cranes or derricks. As the operator moves certain levers, the derrick carries the coils to the iron. Then the operator closes a switch. Electricity can now flow through the coils and make them magnetic. With the strong magnets holding fast to the iron, the.

operator moves the levers again so that the derrick can lift and move the iron to the place where it is needed. There, the switch is opened, the coils cease to be magnetic and the iron is released.

Using Electricity to Send Messages

The scientists who first experimented with electricity had no idea of the thousands of uses that were later to be found for it. Samuel Morse first heard of electromagnets only a little over one hundred years ago. A scientist named Joseph Henry had showed that an electromagnet weighing only 100 pounds could be made to lift over 4000 pounds of iron. This gave Morse an idea. Why not use electricity to send messages?

For a long time, Morse kept thinking of a way to make electricity carry messages over wires. He kept trying experiments for seven years before he found one that worked. In 1837, he applied for a patent on his electromagnetic telegraph. This invention was very simple. It consisted of a small electromagnet which could pull down a piece of iron whenever a key or switch was closed. The key was

IMPROVED TELEGRAPH INSTRUMENTS

connected by wires to the electromagnet and to the electric battery. When attracted by the electromagnet, the piece of iron came down with a "click." That was the signal. For each letter of the alphabet, Morse arranged a different set of clicks. In this way, he was able to spell out words and send messages.

Telegraph keys and sounders similar to those constructed by Morse can be made easily by any boy or girl. All that is needed is a few iron nails, some wire, some strips of metal cut from a tin can, a block of wood and a dry cell. The picture on this page shows how these materials are put together. Be sure to wind at least twenty turns of insulated wire around the nails.

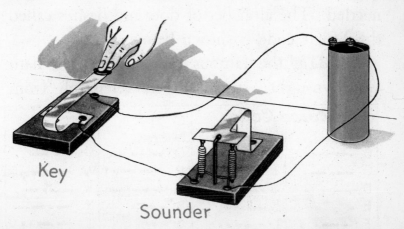

Key

Sounder

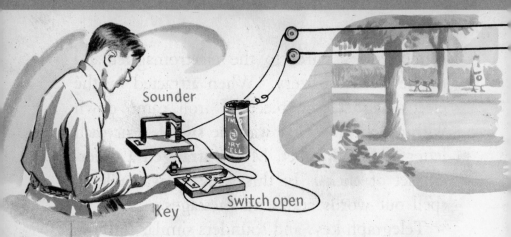

Sounder

Switch open

Key

Each block of wood may contain both a key and a sounder, or the keys and sounders can be made separately. With these telegraph instruments and with wires connecting them, it is easily possible to send telegraphic messages from one room to another or from one house to another. Of course, the greater the distance between sounders, the more dry cells will be needed. The alphabet of dots and dashes called the Morse code is shown below.

In 1844, the famous message, "What hath God wrought," was sent by telegraph from

The Morse Code

A ._	G __.	M __	T _
B _...	H	N _.	U .._
C _._.	I ..	O ___	V ..._
D _..	J .___	P .__.	W .__
E .	K _._	Q __._	X _.._
F .._.	L ._..	R ._.	Y _.__
			S ...	Z __..

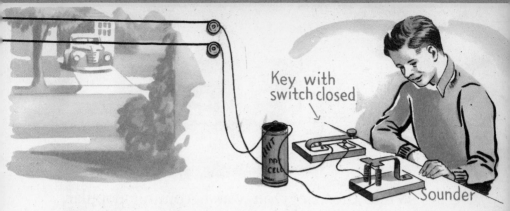

Key with switch closed

Sounder

Baltimore to Washington. The telegraph was a success. Soon additional telegraph lines were built between other cities. That gave Cyrus W. Field an idea. Why not lay a cable across the bottom of the ocean?

Field began to study the best ways of making cable and laying it down in the ocean. When all was ready, a ship loaded with cable set out from Ireland. Over a thousand miles of cable were laid on the ocean bed, and then the cable broke. The next year a different plan was tried. Two ships met in the middle of the ocean. The cable was spliced together, and each ship set out in a different direction. But again the cable broke. Field tried again and again. Finally, in 1866, the cable was successfully laid.

BELL'S
TELEPHONE

While the telegraph was becoming popular, Dr. Alexander Graham Bell began thinking of a way to send the human voice over a wire. This would be much simpler and more convenient than communicating by dots and dashes. The solving of this problem also required several years. But by 1876, Bell had solved it and had taken his newly invented telephone to the Centennial Exposition then being held in Philadelphia. Large crowds gathered to see the new wonder of electricity. Even visitors from foreign countries were interested. One day two

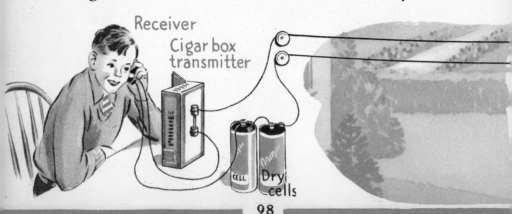

Receiver
Cigar box
transmitter
CELL
Dry
cells

visitors from Japan stopped and inquired if the telephone would talk Japanese. They tried it to find out. Yes, the telephone would even talk Japanese!

When we speak over a telephone, our voice does not actually travel over the wire. A current of electricity travels over the wire. The transmitter of a telephone catches the sound vibrations. These vibrations then cause the electricity to flow in little spurts instead of in a smooth current. The receiver of a telephone contains an electromagnet and a small disk which changes the little spurts of electricity back into sound waves. The diagrams on these pages show how to build a homemade telephone transmitter that works very well, and how to connect these transmitters to receivers so that you can carry on a two-way conversation.

Carbons from dry cells and flashlight cell

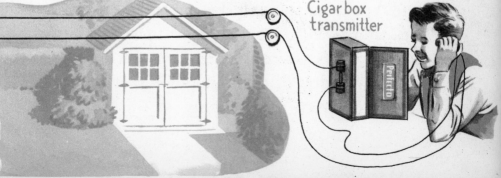

Cigar box transmitter

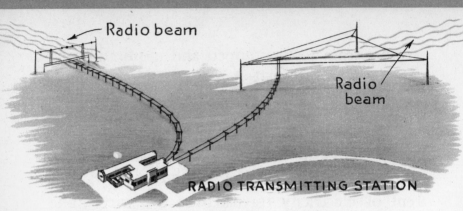

Radio beam

Radio beam

RADIO TRANSMITTING STATION

About the time that the telephone was invented, a German scientist named Hertz discovered radio waves. Twenty years later, Marconi, an Italian, succeeded in using these waves to send messages without wires. Since then many other scientists have made other important discoveries, and our ways of sending messages are still being improved. Today, we can not only send pictures over wires or through the air, but we can make the pictures move and seem to talk. When television was invented, many people thought that the sending of messages could not possibly be improved any further. But now we have television in technicolor. During the years to come, there will be still further wonders of communication that no one has yet dreamed of inventing.

Electricity for Heat and Light

Collect a few samples of different kinds of wire, such as copper, iron, brass and aluminum. Try to get thin wire and thick wire of each kind. Cut off pieces of different lengths, and connect each in turn to the terminals of a dry cell. Do any of the wires become warm? Which metal becomes heated most rapidly? Do thin wires become warmer than thicker wires? Do long wires become warmer than shorter wires? Try the same experiments with two dry cells instead of one. Does that make the wires hotter?

Using electricity to obtain heat makes the burning of fuel unnecessary. It also avoids the bother of ashes or the danger of poisonous gases. That is why electric heating devices are becoming so popular, especially in the home.

Heating Elements
in Toaster

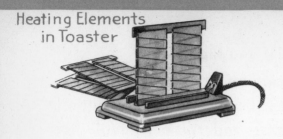

Heating Element
in Iron

There we find electric heating elements in ovens, in toasters, in percolators, in chafing dishes, in irons, in hot plates and in room heaters. Examine some of these devices, and see if you can locate in each of them the wire coil that is heated when electricity flows through it.

When anything becomes hot enough, it glows and gives out light. The hotter it becomes, the brighter it becomes. Edison made use of this fact when he invented the electric lamp. Many scientists before him had thought of the same idea, but they did not succeed in making a lamp that would last very long. If you wish to see what the chief difficulty is, try this experiment:

Attach a piece of thin iron wire, about four inches long, to two nails which stick through a cork. Fit the cork into the neck of a glass bottle. Then connect four dry cells to the heads of the nails. If the iron wire gets hot enough to glow, you will have made an electric lamp. Now see how long it will last. If your lamp is a good one, it should be very bright. In order to be bright, the wire must get very hot. Before long, the iron wire will begin to burn in the air of the bottle; finally it will break, and the lamp will go out.

Edison was faced with the same difficulty. For years, he worked at the problem without favorable results. At last, it occurred to him that the air should be removed from the glass bulb. Then he found that some kinds of wire lasted longer than others. After many years of experimentation, he discovered that the best results were to be had with a thread of carbon. The first successful lamp contained a carbon filament which gave a fairly bright light for about 100 hours.

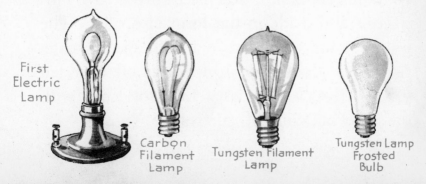

First
Electric
Lamp

Carbon
Filament
Lamp

Tungsten Filament
Lamp

Tungsten Lamp
Frosted
Bulb

Since Edison's time, the electric lamp has been much improved. Today, we use the metal tungsten for the filament wire. Tungsten can be made white hot without melting or burning too rapidly. In many of the modern electric lamps, most of the air is removed and the glass bulbs are filled with some other gas. This makes the lamps last longer and gives the light a brighter hue.

Bright signs of many colors now light up our city streets. They are usually called neon signs because the red ones contain the gas neon. Other gases are used to produce orange, blue, and green lights. Such lamps contain no filaments. Electricity is sent through them under high pressure. This causes the molecules of gas within the tubes to give off light.

Recently, a new kind of electric lamp, called a fluorescent lamp, has been invented. This lamp is also made in the form of a tube. The inside of the tube is coated with special materials. The fluorescent lamp gives off over ten times as much light as a filament lamp with the same amount of current.

The Science Club

The boys and girls in Bill's class at school became very much interested in studying electricity. They decided to form a science club. The club had twenty-four members. It met every week. At each meeting two members performed experiments and explained them.

One week Jack and Betty were on the program for experiments. Jack brought in an electric hot plate, a large tin can, some tubing and a piece of apparatus that looked somewhat like a wheel.

"With this apparatus," began Jack, "I am going to try to show you how a turbine works."

"What's a turbine?" asked John.

"A turbine is a kind of wheel that is turned by water or steam. All the big ocean liners are run by turbines. Turbines are also connected with generators to generate electricity. I am going to use steam to run this turbine."

"Where did you get your turbine?" asked Mary.

"I made it," said Jack. "It was very easy to

make. First, I drove a nail through this piece of board. Next, I heated the end of a piece of glass tubing and closed the end. When the tubing was placed on the nail, it made a very good bearing. I next made a hole in a cork, and slipped it over the tubing. Then I stuck a row of pen points all around the cork."

Jack put some water in the tin can, placed the can on the hot plate and turned on the current.

"If this were a big turbine and were to be used to turn a generator," continued Jack, "the fuel would be either coal or oil. I am going to ask you to imagine that the hot plate is a big coal furnace."

"And the tin can is the boiler," suggested John.

"Yes, and this tubing is the pipe that runs to the turbine."

Jack then placed a short piece of glass tubing in the end of the rubber tube, and adjusted it so that it was near the row of pens. Soon the water began to boil, and steam came out of the tube. The steam struck the pens, and the turbine began to spin rapidly.

"Didn't you say that water can be used to turn turbines, too?" asked Bill.

Jack turned off the electricity and took his turbine over to the faucet. He then removed the stopper and tubing from the can, and connected them with the faucet. When the stream of water was directed against the turbine blades, the turbine turned almost as rapidly as it had done with steam.

"In this case," explained Jack, "the tube is like the penstock of a hydroelectric station. In a hydroelectric station the turbines are near the bottom of the dam. They are connected by long rods to generators placed above them. The generator changes the energy of falling water into electrical energy."

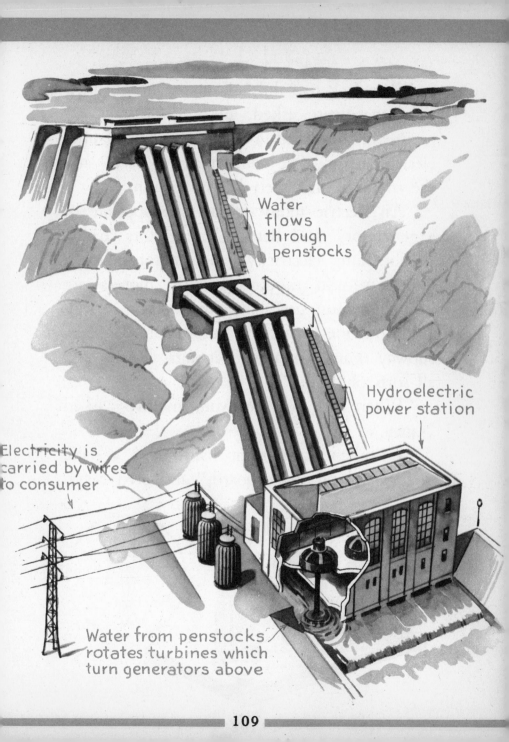

Water
flows
through
penstocks

Hydroelectric
power station

Electricity is
carried by wires
to consumer

Water from penstocks
rotates turbines which
turn generators above

When Jack had finished answering all questions that were asked, Betty began her experiment. She had a dry cell and a little electric motor. She connected the wires, and the motor immediately began to hum.

"An electric motor is just the opposite of a generator," said Betty. "Generators change motion into electricity, and motors change electricity into motion. Electric motors are about the most useful machines in the world. They provide power for factories, trolley cars, subway trains, elevators, vacuum cleaners and all sorts of things."

"Where did you get your motor?" asked Nancy.

"I made it from some nails, wire, a piece of glass tubing and a board," answered Betty.

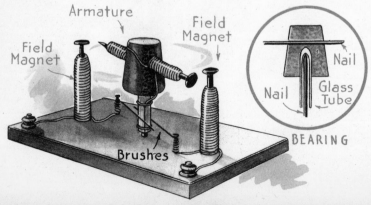

"But how did you know how to put it together?" John inquired.

"I got the plans out of a book," said Betty. "My father helped me make it."

"Do you understand how it works?" asked John.

"Certainly, I understand it," Betty answered. "But it is not easy to explain in words. Explaining how a motor works is like telling someone how to get to a place where he has never been. It seems simple for the person who is doing the telling, but confusing to the person who is being told. When I put my motor together, I had time to think about it and to figure out the use of each part. An electric motor is not nearly as complicated as it looks, and is a lot of fun to build.

"The moving part of my electric motor is an electromagnet. This is called the armature. On either side there are two other electromagnets. These are the field magnets. The wires are wound so that the field magnets attract and repel the ends of the armature, and give it a spinning motion."

"Don't try to explain it further," said John. "I'm going to build a motor, too, and I want to have the fun of figuring it out all by myself."

Just then it was time to close the meeting. The president of the science club thanked Jack and Betty for presenting such excellent experiments, and the children agreed that the meeting had been one of the most interesting they had ever attended.

The Science Fair

By the end of the school term, the science club had made and collected a great many pieces of science apparatus. The closet of the classroom was packed with them. The science table was filled with electromagnets, batteries, telegraph sets, electric motors, bottles, chemicals, magnets and wires. The members of the science club were discussing what they should do with all the apparatus they had used in their experiments.

"I think we ought to have a science fair," said Bill.

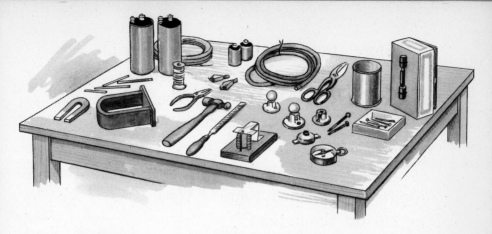

"What's a science fair?" asked several of the members.

"It's a kind of show, or exhibit," explained Bill. "We could arrange our apparatus on tables and have the experiments working. Then we could invite the whole school to come and see them. Perhaps our fathers and mothers would like to come, too."

"But where would we find enough space to do all that?" inquired Nancy.

"I think Room 17 is not being used just now," said Bill. "Maybe we could get permission to have it there."

Everyone thought that this was an excellent idea, and the president of the club said that he would see if he could arrange it.

Before the next meeting of the club, permission had been secured to hold the science fair and to use Room 17. The children all went to this room to make plans for their exhibit.

"But there's already an exhibit in this room," complained John. "What are we going to do about that?"

On the floor in the center of the room were several rows of buildings made of boxes and pasteboard: houses, churches, stores, factories, a police station, a post office and a fire house.

"That belongs to the third grade," explained the president. "They will take it out of the room if we ask them to."

"It seems a pity to spoil their lovely little village," said Mary.

"I have an idea!" cried Frank. "The village is pretty but it is very old-fashioned. It isn't even wired for electricity. There are no lights in the houses, no street lights, or traffic signals. Why don't we put in electricity and bring it up to date?"

"That is an idea!" exclaimed Mary. "Nancy and I will wire the buildings for electricity if someone else will do the street lights."

"John and I will do that," said Frank. "Street lights should be on a different circuit anyway. John and I have plenty of wire and lamps."

"Shouldn't the town have a railroad?" asked Bill. "I could bring my electric train."

"Good!" cried the others, and soon everyone was busily at work.

For several days, Room 17 was the scene of excited activity. Electricians were hard at work running electric circuits through the village. Other workers arranged the experiments on tables at the side of the room. Everything had to be ready and working on the day set for the science fair.

When the day finally came, there were so many visitors that two of the club members had to act as traffic officers to handle the crowd at the door. Others acted as guides and explained the different things that were exhibited. Still others performed experiments and kept the telephones, telegraphs and other pieces of apparatus in working order.

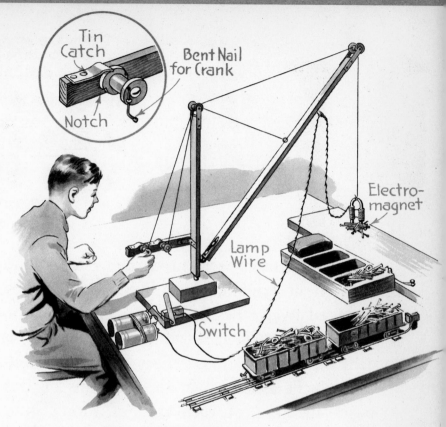

Tin Catch

Bent Nail for Crank

Notch

Electro-magnet

Lamp Wire

Switch

One of the most popular exhibits was Jimmy's derrick and lifting magnet. The picture shows exactly how it was made and how it worked. Jimmy loaded small pieces of iron on a toy railroad car. By moving the derrick and turning the switch on and off at the proper times, the pieces of iron did not have to be touched by hand.

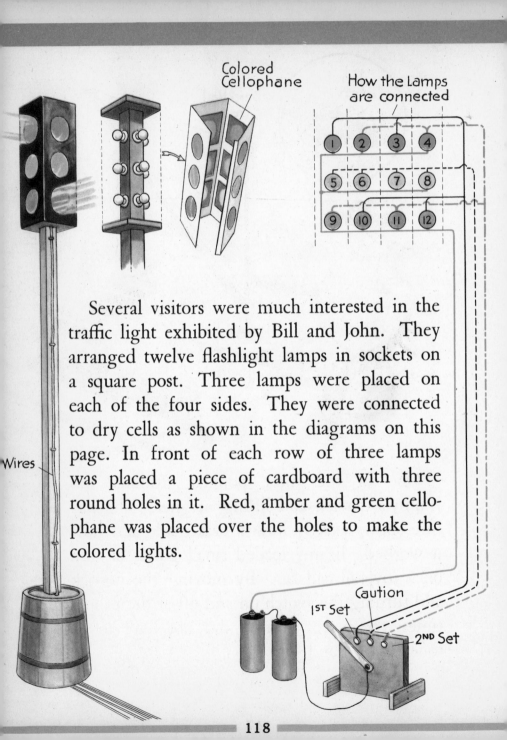

Colored Cellophane

How the Lamps are connected

1	2	3	4
5	6	7	8
9	10	11	12

Wires

Several visitors were much interested in the traffic light exhibited by Bill and John. They arranged twelve flashlight lamps in sockets on a square post. Three lamps were placed on each of the four sides. They were connected to dry cells as shown in the diagrams on this page. In front of each row of three lamps was placed a piece of cardboard with three round holes in it. Red, amber and green cellophane was placed over the holes to make the colored lights.

Caution

1ST Set

2ND Set

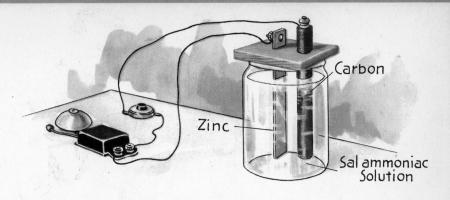

Margaret had made an electric cell that would ring a bell. A wooden cover with two holes in it was placed over a pint jar as shown. Four ounces of sal ammoniac were placed in the jar, and the jar was filled with water. The carbon rod was obtained from an old dry cell.

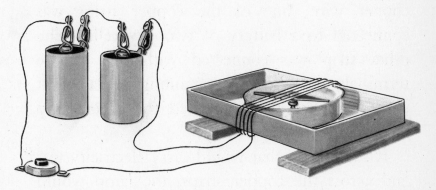

With the above apparatus Jack showed that a current of electricity flowing through a coil of wire would move the compass needle.

George exhibited a tester that he had made. The tester consisted of two strips of copper fastened to a piece of board. By means of a copper wire, one of the copper strips was connected to a battery of two dry cells. The other strip was connected with one of the terminals of a socket containing a flashlight lamp. A wire also connected the other lamp terminal with the battery.

If something that would carry electricity was laid across the copper strips, the lamp would light. A piece of wire was attached to each copper strip so that liquids, as well as solids, could be tested.

Frances exhibited her homemade lamp socket. It was made of a piece of copper wire coiled so that a flashlight lamp could be screwed into the coil. This was fastened to a wooden base. Another piece of copper wire was also fastened to the base so that it would make contact with the end terminal of the lamp.

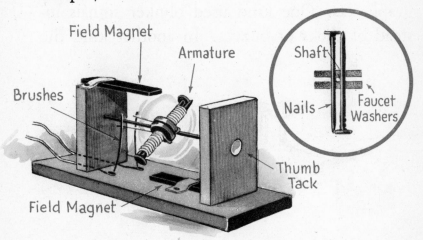

Robert showed an electric motor that he had made.

There were many different kinds of telegraph sets. One kind used blinker signals instead of clicks or buzzes. In another kind the

key and the sounder were built on the same base.

Back of cardboard

QUESTIONS	ANSWERS
1 • What is the Stone?	A flare chrem one •
2 • When did it first?	September 1911 •
3 • How is it made?	By election one •
4 • What you a thue?	Sixly are yours •
5 • Why was it hard?	Because a hural •
6 • Whose don't in?	The pnow thru mi •
7 • What non chew?	The Commellara •
8 • Why in not chu?	Has an the run •
9 • When was alona?	In the you an •
10 • How chem an mi?	By Mank n q mi •

When the visitors had seen all the exhibits, they were each given a test on the electric question and answer machine. The pointer was moved to the number of a question and the visitor was asked to place a metal pointer on the button nearest the answer. If the answer was correct, the bell would ring. The above diagram shows how the machine is made.

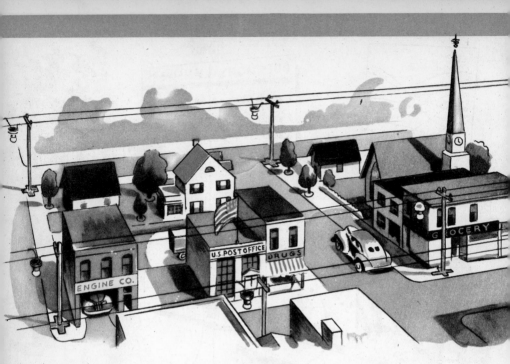

The biggest exhibit at the science fair was, of course, the village. Lights shone from the windows of many of the houses. Trains rushed by the station and signals blinked. The street lamps lighted the streets clearly.

The visitors who came to the science fair had an enjoyable time. But the boys and girls who worked at the fair had a still better time. When the fair was over it was not forgotten. Everyone talked about it for days, and kept on asking and answering questions about the different things at the fair.

Topics for Further Study

Things to Do

1. Learn to connect bells, lamps, buzzers and other devices with one and two dry cells.
2. Make a crystal radio receiver.
3. Learn to figure the cost of operating electric lamps and other devices.
4. Make a burglar alarm that will ring a bell when a door is opened.
5. Learn to read an electric meter.
6. Examine electric lamps of different sizes, and notice the wattage of each. Learn to figure the cost of operating electric lamps for different periods of time. (Electricity is sold by the kilowatt hour. One kilowatt-hour equals 1000 watt-hours.)
7. Make an electric bell.
8. Make an electric sparkler like the one shown below.

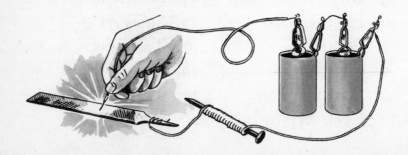

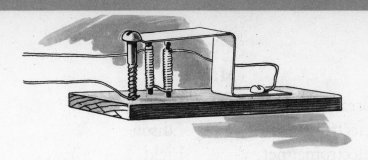

9. Make a buzzer like the one shown above.
10. Report on the work of Marconi, De Forest, Edison and others who have made important discoveries about electricity.
11. Use the tester shown on page 120 to find out whether water will conduct electricity. Now put salt in the water and test again.

Some of the following statements are true. Others can be corrected by changing one word. Copy all the statements so that each is true.

1. Electromagnets should be wound with *bare* copper wire.
2. The moving part of an electric motor is called the *armature*.
3. The receiver of a telephone contains an *electromagnet*.
4. When we talk over a telephone, *sound* travels over the wires.

Match

ocean cable   Bell
electric lamp   Edison
electromagnet   Field
radio waves   Henry
telegraph   Hertz
telephone   Morse

Questions

1. How can you make an electromagnet?
2. How does an electromagnet differ from a bar magnet?
3. How would you increase the strength of an electromagnet?
4. What is insulated wire?
5. Why must the wire used in electromagnets be insulated?
6. What metal is usually used in the wire of an electromagnet?
7. What metal is usually used for the core of an electromagnet?
8. For what different purposes do we use electricity?

THE WORLD OF SOUND

Ceremony in Buffalo

Ceremony in New York Bay

SENECA CHIEF

Vibrations in the Air

From Buffalo to Albany and from Albany to New York, people were bustling with excitement. It was October 26, 1825. The Erie Canal had been completed and was about to be opened. Careful plans had been made to spread the news. All along the route from Buffalo to New York City, cannon had been placed on hilltops several miles apart.

As the boats carrying De Witt Clinton and his party entered the canal at Buffalo, the first cannon was fired. Several seconds later the sound of this cannon was heard a few miles away by the men who were waiting to fire the second cannon. All the way from Buffalo to New York, cannon after cannon boomed out. Within an hour and twenty minutes, in New York City the last cannon announced the joining of the waters of Lake Erie with those of the Atlantic Ocean.

In 1883 came another famous event in the history of sound. Krakatoa, a volcano on an island in the Indian Ocean, exploded. This explosion was probably the loudest sound ever heard on earth. Great pieces of rock and large quantities of dust and ashes were hurled more than seventeen miles into the air, and the sky was darkened for several days. The sound was heard clearly in Africa, Asia and Australia at distances as great as three thousand miles from the scene of the explosion. Winds of hurricane force continued for six weeks. Waves over fifty feet high swept across the oceans and were felt as far away as Cape Horn, a distance of nearly eight thousand miles.

The firing of cannon and the explosions of volcanoes cause vibrations of the air that we hear as sounds. Many kinds of sounds are caused by other objects that shake and tremble. Leaves rustle in the wind, branches break and fall. A wandering insect buzzes, or a bee hums as he flits from flower to flower. Grasshoppers chirp, owls hoot and frogs croak.

One sometimes hears the sound of the babbling brook, the songs of birds, the lowing of cattle and even perhaps the squeak of a mouse. If a storm comes up, there is the howl of the wind and the crash of thunder. Near the ocean there is the roar of the sea.

In the city, different and often less pleasant sounds reach our ears. The radiators hiss, bells ring, trucks rumble, trolley cars clang and subway trains rattle their way along the tracks. Where buildings are under construction or roadways under repair, sledge-hammers deliver their blows with nerve-racking sounds. The grinding gears of heavy buses and the screeching brakes of cars add more sounds. At night, radios blare from open windows or through the thin walls between apartments. There is no such thing as complete quiet anywhere in a world full of movement.

It will be interesting to begin our study of sound by doing a number of simple experiments. Hold your fingers lightly against your throat and hum or say "a-a-a-ah." Do you feel the quivering in the windpipe? The vocal cords are vibrating.

Tap on an iron rod or piece of pipe as you touch it lightly with your fingers. Can you feel the vibration?

Stretch a rubber band with one end held between your teeth, and pluck the rubber band. You can see the vibrations and hear the sound.

Strike the prongs of a tuning fork sharply on the table and then bring them to your ear. What do you hear? Now grip the prongs in the palm of your hand. What do you feel? Strike the tuning fork again and plunge the ends into a jar of water. What makes the water spatter in all directions?

Place a small cork on the head of a drum and strike the drum lightly with the stick. Note how the cork jumps into the air. The vibrating drumhead threw it off.

Try to get music out of a saw by gripping the handle between your knees, bending the blade slightly at the end and striking the middle with a drumstick. Can you play a tune?

Swish the blackboard pointer through the air. What causes the sound? Try the same thing with a short, thin stick and a longer, thicker stick. Is there any difference in the sounds made?

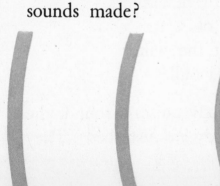

Blow at an angle over the top of a narrow-mouthed bottle. What vibrates in this case?

Touch a violin as it is being played. Do you feel the vibrations? Can you notice the vibration of some object in the room when the radio is being played loudly?

All of these experiments lead to one conclusion: sounds are produced by vibrating objects. Here are a number of well-known sounds. Can you tell in each case what it is that vibrates to make the sound?

The crack of a whip
The slamming of a door
The clapping of hands
The rustling of silk
The screech of automobile brakes
The pitapat of raindrops
The creaking of new shoes
The splashing of water
The whistle of the wind
The whine of a bullet

When a vibrating body causes a sound, the air particles near the body are disturbed. They

disturb other air particles near by; these in turn disturb their neighbors and so on. Before long, air particles far removed from the sounding body are also disturbed.

Arrange four rows of wooden dominoes or toy blocks as shown in the picture above. Tip over the inside blocks by pushing down with a rubber ball. Each block, in falling, will tip over the next block, which will in turn tip over the next. Soon, the disturbance travels down the line in all directions until the last blocks fall down. If you had enough blocks to make each row a mile long, the disturbance caused by the ball might travel a mile in each direction. If it were possible to line up 100 rows, all centering at the ball, the push of the ball would move out in 100 different directions.

The vibrations of a sounding body travel through the air in the same way. The disturbance is handed on from air particle to air particle in every direction outward from the sounding body. Test this method of sound travel by placing a ticking clock in the center of the room and walking away from it. Does the sound decrease in loudness as you get farther away? Go back to the clock and walk in another direction. Does the same thing happen? Try walking away in other directions. Do sounds travel in all directions away from the vibrating object?

How Sounds Differ

Of course, all sounds are not alike. The howl of the wind is not like the creak of a door or the musical tones of a violin. Even the sounds from the same kind of vibrating object can differ. In the case of the musical instrument, some of the tones are high and some are low. In fact, one can play or sing a series of tones from very low to very high, each tone higher than the one which precedes it, and not quite so high as the one that follows. We can go up a musical scale just as we can climb the steps of a ladder. The word pitch is used to describe the highness or the lowness of a tone.

Play a phonograph record of a singing voice, allowing the motor to turn the disk at the proper speed. Increase the speed and notice the change in pitch. Decrease the speed and notice the change in pitch.

Hold a card against the spokes of a bicycle wheel and turn the wheel slowly. Listen to the sound made as the card raps against the spokes. Now turn the wheel faster and listen to the same sound again. Notice that it is higher in pitch.

From these experiments and others of the same kind, it would seem that the pitch of a sound depends upon the number of vibrations per second. The more vibrations per second, the higher is the pitch.

Lift the hinged board of a piano and study the steel strings inside. When the keys are pressed, felt-covered hammers strike the strings, causing them to vibrate and to give out musical sounds. Some of the strings are long and thick; they give the low tones. Others are very short and thin; they give the high tones. The shorter the string, the higher the tone.

In addition to changing the length and thickness of a string, there is another way of altering the pitch of its sound. A piano tuner uses a wrench to turn the pegs to which the piano strings are fastened. In this way he can lessen or increase the tension on the string. The tighter he pulls the string, the higher is the pitch. The piano tuner tightens or loosens the strings one by one, until all the different tones follow each other properly up and down the musical scale.

If you have ever tried to play a violin or if you have watched someone playing a violin, you know that this instrument also has thick strings and thin strings. Again, the thicker strings give the lower pitched tones. Also, the pegs on a violin allow the player to tighten or loosen the strings so as to tune the instrument properly. When playing a tune, the violinist presses his fingers down upon the strings at different points. In this way, he changes the length of string, producing the different-pitched tones needed for the melody.

You may be interested in making a piano. Obtain a large assortment of pins or nails, varying in thickness and in length. Drive them into a board in order of size. They give out musical tones when plucked or struck. If you are painstaking and have a good ear for music, you can "tune" the pins or nails so that they will follow the musical scale of a piano. You will notice that the pitch of any nail can be

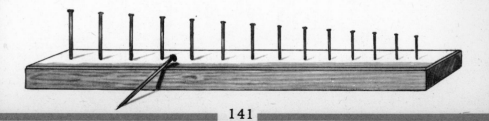

raised by driving it deeper into the board. That makes the vibrating part of the nail shorter. To lower the pitch of a nail, pull it up with the claw of a hammer.

Another kind of toy musical instrument can be made with a series of test tubes. Mount them in a block of wood as shown in the picture. Pour different amounts of water into each tube. By blowing air across the top of a test tube, the column of air inside is set in vibration and makes a musical tone. The shorter the air column, the higher is the pitch of the tone. The different tones can therefore be tuned properly by pouring in just the right amount of water into each tube. A medicine dropper is useful for adding or taking out water, drop by drop. The best means for blowing air across the tops of the air columns is a long tube, flattened at one end.

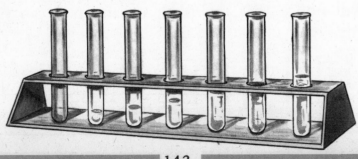

Can the pitch of a sounding string be changed by plucking it harder or more softly? Try it with the strings of a piano and a violin. Try it with your nail-piano. You will find in each case that the sound is louder when you pluck harder, but the pitch remains the same. If bits of paper are hung on a string, hard plucking of the string will make them jump into the air. The hard-plucked string swings back and forth through a greater distance, and so can give the paper riders a harder jolt. Gentle plucking causes the string to swing through much less space. This gives a tone that is less loud. However, whether loud or soft, the pitch of the tone remains the same.

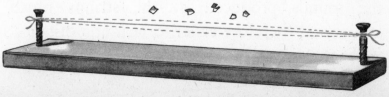

A string which vibrates 256 times in one second gives a tone which is like the tone of middle C on the piano. Striking, bowing or plucking such a string harder will make it move back and forth through a greater distance; but it will continue to vibrate 256 times a second. The only way to change the pitch of a string is to change its length or its tension.

Feel your throat when you are speaking softly; then feel it when you make a loud sound. The vocal cords vibrate through a greater distance when you talk loudly, even though the pitch of the sounds you make remains the same.

If a vibrating string is fastened to a board, the board vibrates also. Since the board is in contact with a great deal of air, the vibrating board produces a much larger air-ripple than the string alone could have produced. That is why pianos have sounding boards. They make the sounds produced by the strings much louder and therefore easier to hear at a distance.

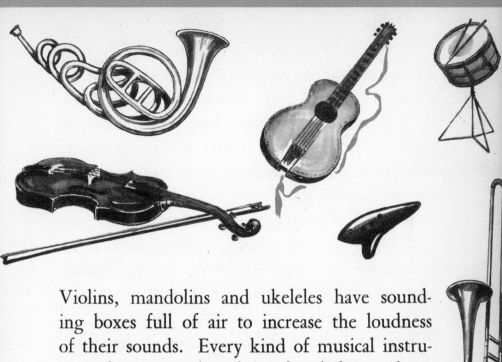

Violins, mandolins and ukeleles have sounding boxes full of air to increase the loudness of their sounds. Every kind of musical instrument has a sounding box of a different shape and size. In radio loud-speakers and phonographs, air is caused to vibrate by means of a disk. In this way, a large amount of air is set in motion, and the loudness of the sound is increased.

Strike the prongs of a tuning fork and listen for the sound. Then touch the base of the fork to a table top or to a door. How do you account for the greater loudness of the sound you hear?

If you were to shut your eyes and listen to a musical tone played first by a violin, then by a piano, then by a saxophone and finally sung by a person, you would have no trouble in guessing which instrument was being used. The pitch and loudness in each case might be the same, and yet there would somehow be a difference. To explain this difference, we say that tones have a certain quality, as well as pitch and loudness. In order to understand what causes the difference in quality of sounds, we must realize that objects can vibrate at different speeds at the same time. It has been shown that a string may vibrate as a whole 256 times a second. At the same time, the two halves of the same string are also vibrating 512 times a second. The sound we hear best is that which comes from the string when it is vibrating as a whole, but partial vibrations are heard to some extent. The two kinds of vibrations together give the sound its quality.

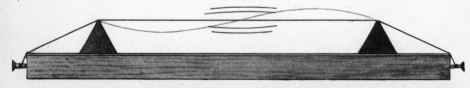

PARTIAL VIBRATION

When the main vibrations and the lesser ones harmonize pleasantly, the sound produced has a good quality. If vibrations do not blend well, the quality of sound is poor. We may even refer to such a sound as a noise. A cigarbox fiddle does not sound as well as a real violin. The material of the strings and sounding box, the shape and the size, and even the kind of lacquer or varnish used all affect the kind and number of lesser vibrations.

A violin constructed in the eighteenth century by the famous Stradivarius family may cost $50,000; a violin of some other make may cost only $5. Stradivarius knew the secret of building violins whose lesser vibrations blended beautifully with the main vibrations.

This difference in quality is to be found also in the human voice. The reason we can recognize our friends by the sound of their voices is because no two sets of vocal cords vibrate exactly alike.

VOCAL CORDS

Speaking   Breathing

How Sounds Travel

If a sound is to travel from one place to another, there must be some kind of material to carry the wave. Sounds can travel easily through solid materials and through water as well as through the air. As a matter of fact, solids and liquids are better carriers of sound waves than air. This may be shown in the following way.

Get a long stick of wood and let your friend hold one end of it to his ear. Holding the other end in your hand, scratch the stick gently with a pencil. Does your friend hear the sound? See how tiny a noise you must make before your friend reports that he does not hear it. Evidently, wood carries sounds more readily than air does, because your friend can hear a light scratch through the stick, but he cannot hear the same noise through the air.

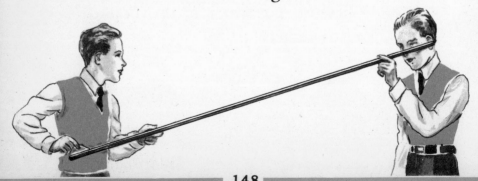

Now get two pieces of wood and hold the ends about one quarter of an inch apart. The quarter-inch air gap stops most of the sound vibrations. Try the same experiment with metal rods or pipes.

Water is one of the best carriers of sound. Some day when you are swimming under water, click two stones together very gently. You will be surprised at the loudness of the sound. Your friends, if they also happen to have their heads under water, will report that they heard a loud, knocking sound. Sounds made in water have been known to travel for miles without decreasing much in loudness.

It is easy to make a string telephone like the one shown in the picture. Take two pillboxes or tin cans and punch a hole in the center of each. Connect them with a string or thread stretched tightly. See if you can carry on a conversation through this telephone.

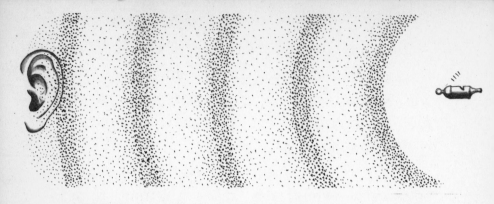

When sounds travel through substances, the disturbance caused by a vibrating object passes on from one particle of the substance to another. Of course, this takes some time, though not very much. Scientists have measured very carefully how fast sound waves travel through air and through many other materials. In one second, a sound wave will travel about 1000 feet in air, about 5000 feet in water and about 16,000 feet in steel.

Although such speeds seem very great, the speed of light is much greater. Did you ever watch a ball game from the grandstand? First, you see the man at bat hit the ball. Then, when the ball is flying through the air, the sound of the ball meeting the bat reaches your ears.

In an electric storm, we usually see the lightning flash several seconds before we hear the thunder. Yet we know that the flash and the crash occurred at the same instant. People sometimes count the number of seconds that pass from the time they see the lightning until they hear the thunder. In that way, they can estimate the distance to the storm. If they count five seconds, it means that the lightning flashed about one mile away.

Echoes are reflected sounds. Sounds may travel through the air until they strike a high wall or a mountain, and then bounce back like a rubber ball. There is a tall story about a man in the Swiss Alps who always shouted out the window when he went to bed. He related that the echo returned at just the right time to wake him up in the morning. Though

this story was much exaggerated, there are places where remarkable echoes actually are heard. Near an ancient tomb in Rome, it is possible to recite an entire verse of poetry and to hear it again a few seconds later exactly as it was spoken. Echoes of explosions are known to have traveled distances as great as fifty miles.

Echoes have been put to practical use in finding the depths of the ocean. This is done by exploding a bomb near a ship and counting the time required for the sound wave to travel to the ocean bottom and back again.

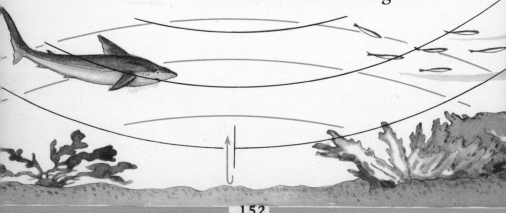

How Sounds Are Heard

We have learned how sounds are made, how they may differ in pitch, in loudness and in quality, and how they travel through air and other materials. Let us now see what happens when sound waves reach the ear. What you see when you look into a mirror is only the outer part of the ear. This looks like a funnel. It is useful for collecting sound waves.

After the sounds are gathered by the outer ear, the waves pass into a channel and strike against the eardrum. This is a very thin membrane which vibrates when the air waves strike it. It vibrates in a manner similar to that of the vibrating object which started the sound wave.

Beyond the eardrum is the middle ear which contains three small bones. One of them rests against the eardrum, and is called the hammer. The hammer rests against a second bone, called the anvil. Both bones carry the vibrations to another bone, which is stirrup-shaped and rests against an oval-shaped drum.

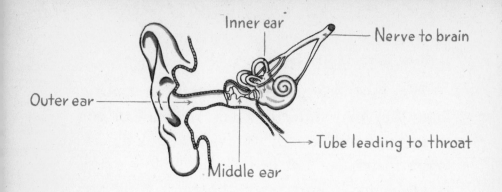

Inner ear

Nerve to brain

Outer ear

Tube leading to throat

Middle ear

This drum carries the vibrations to the inner ear, which is shaped like a snail-shell and is filled with a fluid. The vibrations in the fluid sweep by a series of nerve-endings. The nerves lead to the brain. We do not know exactly what happens from this point on. However, we do know that the vibrations stimulate the nerves, and that when the nerve message reaches the brain, we hear a sound.

Since our ears are very complicated and delicate, we should take good care of them. A very loud sound may cause the eardrum to break. That is why soldiers frequently plug their ears with soft cotton when they are close to a firing cannon. Boxing a person's ears is a dangerous practice; it may injure the middle ear. Diving to a great depth in water is also dangerous. The pressure of water may fill the ear channels and interfere with good hearing.

Be careful how you blow your nose. Violent nose-blowing may strain the eardrums and force germs into the ears. Keep your ears clean to lessen the chance of infection. If wax accumulates in your ears, do not try to pick it out. That should be done by a doctor who knows how to soften the wax and to remove it. The soft wax which is constantly being secreted in the outer ear is really a protection against dust and other foreign particles, which might get in and interfere with the vibrations of the eardrum.

The human ear is tuned to pick up sounds ranging from 16 to 20,000 vibrations per second. Beyond these limits there are many sounds we cannot hear. Some insects communicate with each other with sounds as high as 32,000 vibrations per second. We hear only the lower notes of the hummingbird's song, but not the higher notes. At times the throat of a hummingbird swells and its bill moves, but the pitch of its song is too high for us to

hear. Many other birds, mice and insects produce sounds so high in pitch that we never hear them at all.

Recently scientists have found some interesting uses for sounds of very high pitch. After being exposed to high frequency sounds for a few minutes, eggs will keep fresh for many months without refrigeration. With one kind of sound, the temperature of eggs can be raised to the point where they will be boiled. Bacteria can also be killed by sounds of a very high pitch. The rapid vibrations of such sound shake the bacteria apart.

High frequency sounds are now used to detect the presence of submarines and icebergs. Sounds made by special instruments are reflected back like an echo from the submarine or iceberg, whose exact location can thus be determined.

Things to Do

1. Make a list of all the sounds that you hear in ten minutes of a class period. Tell what vibrates in each case.
2. Hold a small pillow on your finger tips in a room where someone is playing the piano. Do you feel the pillow vibrate?
3. Learn to play "America" on a set of drinking glasses, properly "tuned" with water.
4. Learn to make a water tumbler "sing" by rubbing its rim with a moistened finger.
5. Make a cigar-box violin.
6. Tap one end of a metal pipe and have someone listen with his ear to the other end.
7. Make a telephone with tin cans and string.
8. Have someone play the same note on different instruments. Without looking, try to guess which instrument is being played.
9. Test different substances such as iron, wood, a slate blackboard, cement and paper to see which ones carry sound best.
10. Find out how sound-proof rooms are constructed; prepare a report for your class.

Topics for Further Study

1. Bagpipes	11. Sirens
2. Bells	12. Stradivarius
3. Brass instruments	13. Stethoscopes
4. Chords	14. String instruments
5. Cuckoo clocks	
6. Katydids	15. Swiss yodelers
7. Krakatoa	16. Supersonics
8. Microphones	17. Television
9. Percussion instruments	18. Whispering
	19. Xylophones
10. Radio sound effects	20. Zithers

Each statement below may be completed by adding one word. The correct word may or may not be among those suggested.

1. Reflected sounds are called
   keys   explosions   . . . .
2. Middle C vibrates 256 times per
   second   minute   . . . .
3. Sound travels about 1000 feet per second in
   water   steel   . . . .
4. Shortening a vibrating string raises the
   echo   pitch   . . . .

WONDERS OF THE SKY

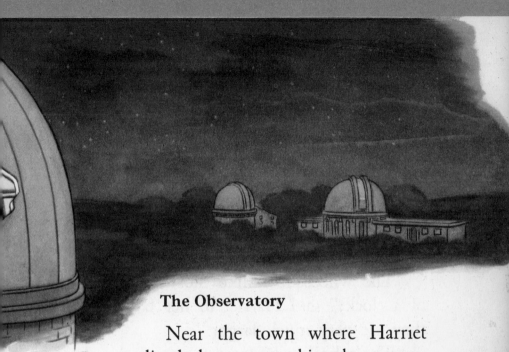

The Observatory

Near the town where Harriet lived there was a big observatory. The observatory had three large telescopes, each covered by a great dome. Scientists used these telescopes to study the stars and planets.

Every Wednesday evening a part of the observatory was open for visitors. Harriet and her father often went to the observatory on Wednesday nights when the sky was clear. They climbed up a winding stairway in one of the towers of the observatory. At the top of the stairway, in a large circular room, was the great telescope. Harriet and her father took their turns with the other visitors in looking through the telescope. An astronomer kept the telescope adjusted, answered the visitors' questions and told many interesting facts about the heavenly bodies.

One evening, while waiting for her turn to look at the stars, Harriet looked through the glass window at the base of the telescope. She could see many turning wheels.

"The wheels look like those on the inside of a clock," said Harriet to her father, "only they are very much larger."

"The wheels you see are part of the clock-work of the telescope," said her father. "They turn the telescope at just the right speed."

"But why must the telescope keep turning?"

"Have you forgotten that the stars remain fixed in their places while we are turning around with the earth?" asked Father.

"Oh, I see," said Harriet; "if the telescope did not move, the stars would sail right across the field of the telescope and we could not keep looking at any one of them for long. As we turn eastward with the earth, the upper end

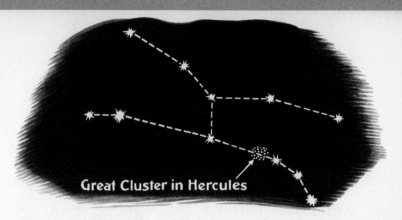
Great Cluster in Hercules

of the telescope must move westward." Just then it was Harriet's turn at the telescope.

"You are now looking at one of the most interesting objects in the heavens," said the astronomer; "the great star cluster in the constellation Hercules. To the naked eye, this cluster looks like a very faint single star. However, even a small telescope shows it to be made up of many stars. Since the sky is quite clear tonight, several hundred stars can be seen. In the center of the cluster they appear so close together that it is impossible to count them. Some of the best photographs of this cluster show over 30,000 separate stars. These stars are suns, billions of miles apart. They seem close together because they are far away. Some of them are two hundred times as bright as our sun.

"The Great Cluster in Hercules is between thirty and forty thousand light years distant from the earth. This means that the light that is now entering the telescope started on its journey to the earth thirty or forty thousand years ago, when the place where this observatory stands was covered by a great glacier.

"We astronomers use the term light years when speaking of star distances, because if the distances were given in miles the numbers would be entirely too large. Light travels 186,000 miles per second. The number of miles in a light year can be found by multiplying 186,000 by the number of seconds in a year. The distance in miles to the Great Cluster in Hercules is roughly 30,000 times the number of miles in a light year."

When everyone had seen the Great Cluster in Hercules the astronomer said, "Now, suppose we look at something close by. We should be able to see Jupiter and his moons clearly tonight. Jupiter is now on the same side of the sun that the earth is—only about 400 million miles away from the earth. At an average

speed of 100 miles per hour, it would require a little less than 500 years to go there, but light travels from Jupiter to the earth in about 40 minutes."

The astronomer turned some switches and pushed some buttons. The great telescope swung around until it pointed to a different place in the sky. The dome over the telescope also turned so that the opening came to the right place.

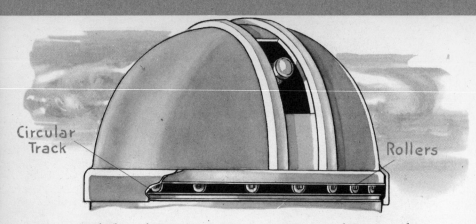

Circular Track

Rollers

While the astronomer was making other adjustments, Harriet asked how it was possible to make the whole dome turn.

"The dome rests on rollers which roll around a track," replied her father. "Electric motors furnish the energy to move the dome into the right position."

After looking at the tiny pin-points of light that came from distant stars, Harriet was pleasantly surprised when she saw Jupiter. It hung in the sky like a beautiful yellow balloon. Darker colored bands were seen around the widest part. The top and bottom seemed to be flattened. Four moons were seen near by.

After everyone had seen Jupiter, the astronomer next pointed out a comet. The comet was a small one, but the tail could be seen

clearly. After that the visitors looked at the moon, and saw the great craters and the dark shadows of mountains that make up the "man in the moon."

Before Harriet and her father left, the astronomer explained that the instrument they had been using was called a refracting telescope. Such a telescope has a large lens at the upper end of the tube and a small lens at the lower end of the tube. The large lens gathers a great deal of light and brings it together near the small lens. The effect is the same as if the pupils of our eyes were enlarged several hundred times.

The astronomer also pointed out another interesting fact. He said that everything seen through a telescope is inverted, and he suggested the following experiment. Get a small magnifying glass and a large magnifying glass. Hold the small one a short distance from your eye and the large one at about arm's length. Now look at something a few hundred feet away. The object at which you look will appear larger than it is and upside down.

"Are there other telescopes in the observatory besides this one?" asked Harriet.

"Yes," said the astronomer; "there are two others, each under a separate dome. But they are reflecting telescopes instead of refracting telescopes. A reflecting telescope has a large

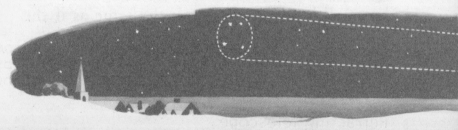

concave mirror at the bottom, instead of a lens. When turned toward the sky, this mirror gathers and reflects any light that strikes it, and the beams of light are brought together near the upper end. The observer rides around on a seat near the upper end.

"Reflecting telescopes can be built much larger than refractors, but are better suited for research work than for observations by visitors. Today most research in astronomy is done by photography rather than by direct observation. The photographic plate is more sensitive than the human eye. Photography also enables astronomers to keep exact records of their observations.

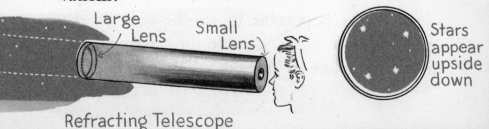

Large Lens   Small Lens   Stars appear upside down

Refracting Telescope

THE TWO-HUNDRED INCH TELESCOPE AT MT. PALOMAR

"Another fact that you may be interested in knowing is that a great deal of astronomical work is now carried on in the daytime. The sky is just as full of stars in the daytime as it is at night, but only the very brightest stars can be seen in the daytime because of the intense light of the sun. With a telescope, however, it is possible to see the stars by day as well as by night, because the telescope tube shuts out most of the sun's light."

Sky Movies

Not long after her visit to the observatory, Harriet went with her father and mother on a trip to the city. In the evening, she suggested that, since there were so many movie theaters in the city, there might be a good show at one of them.

"I think I know a movie you would like," said her father. "The name of the theater is the Planetarium, and the show begins at eight o'clock."

After dinner Harriet and her father started. It seemed to Harriet that the movie was a long distance away. But finally they arrived. The movie theater was different from any Harriet had ever seen. The top was a great dome like the one at the observatory, only there was no opening in the roof and no telescope. They found their seats and waited.

A Planetarium

"This is a queer theater," said Harriet. "Where's the screen?"

"On the ceiling," said her father.

At eight o'clock the lights in the theater began to grow dim. The sun and the moon moved across the dome, just as they do in the real sky. Harriet was very much excited. She wondered what kind of show this was going to be.

When the sun set in the west, the stars came out, and the dome seemed to rise and disappear. The stars were all in their places and gleaming brightly, just as they do when one looks at the sky on a dark night. There was a murmur of surprise from the hundreds of people, and a lecturer in the center of the room began speaking.

The lecturer first pointed out that the stars were moving more rapidly than they appear to move in the real sky, and that it was possible to make them move still faster. Now Harriet could see that there was a machine in the center of the room, which threw beams of light on the ceiling. Each beam made a star.

There was a click of an electric switch, and the stars streaked through the sky and disappeared below the western horizon, only to reappear soon at the eastern horizon. The planetarium stars were made to move across the sky 1000 times as fast as they actually seem to move.

North Star

In the northern sky the stars did not rise and set. Instead, they traveled in great circles, always above the horizon. The only star in the whole sky that did not move was the North Star. The lecturer explained this by saying that if the axis of the earth were extended in a straight line from the North Pole, it would pass very close to the North Star. For this reason, the North Star seems to be stationary as we look at the northern sky from the rotating earth. Near-by stars seem to move around the North Star in small circles, and stars farther away move around it in larger circles. The stars still farther away move in such large circles that part of their paths are below the horizon. There are many stars that cannot be seen in the Northern Hemisphere. To show this the lecturer turned the planetarium instrument so that the audience could "visit" the Southern Hemisphere. When he did this, the North Star and all the other stars near it moved down out of sight below the northern horizon. There was no star above the South Pole, but the Southern Cross and all the other stars of the Southern Hemisphere seemed to move around a point in the sky where the South Star would be if there were one.

When the show ended Harriet was surprised that an entire hour had passed so quickly. She told her father that it had been one of the best "movie" shows she had ever seen. The stars of the sky had been as fine movie actors as any of the stars of Hollywood.

An Umbrella Planetarium

Stars and Constellations

After her visit to the observatory and the planetarium, Harriet became greatly interested in astronomy. By studying sky maps, she learned the names of many of the stars. With a pair of opera glasses and the telescope she got for Christmas, she was able to see some of the planets distinctly. On clear, moonless nights she sometimes took pictures of star trails.

A very interesting star-trail picture can be made by fastening a camera to a solid support and pointing it in the direction of the North Star. The shutter of the camera should then be opened and left open for several hours. To get long star trails in the picture, the best plan is to adjust the camera and go to bed. But be careful to set the alarm clock so that you can get up and close the shutter before the sun's light spoils the picture in the morning. If you are lucky, you may be able to get a picture of the bright trail of a meteor as it crosses the star trails.

Getting acquainted with stars is much like getting acquainted with people. The first thing we wish to know about people and stars is their names. All the brightest stars were named centuries ago; many of them have Arabian names. The shepherds of ancient times had a great deal of time to watch the stars and study them. They talked about the stars as shepherds talk about their sheep; the seven planets then known were the "old sheep stars" and the other stars were grouped in different heavenly "flocks." "The star of the shepherds of the heavenly herds" was the bright star Arcturus. Aldebaran, another bright star, means "the hindmost" in Arabian. It probably was given this name because it was the last sheep in one of the heavenly "flocks."

Stars, like people, are also identified by their addresses. Today, as in ancient times, stars are divided into groups called constellations. The arrangements of the stars within the constellations have suggested the forms of animals, people and gods. Accordingly they were given such names as Taurus, the Bull; Orion, the Hunter; and Cassiopeia, the Lady in the Chair. In all there are 88 different constellations or groups of stars. It will be necessary to learn only a few of these in order to get acquainted with most of the brighter stars in the sky.

The Big Dipper may be used as a starting point in locating the other constellations. The real name of this group of stars is Ursa Major, or the Great Bear. The two stars opposite the handle of the Big Dipper are the pointers. They point to the North Star. Since the stars in the northern sky appear to move around the North Star, it must be remembered that the position of the Dipper changes with the time of night and the season of the year. In the early evening during the winter months, the handle of the Big Dipper points downward.

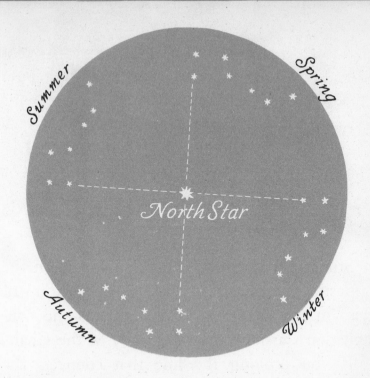

During spring evenings, the handle points toward the east. On summer evenings it points upward, and in the fall it points toward the west.

Having found the Great Bear, one can easily find the Little Bear, or Little Dipper. The North Star is at the end of the handle of the Little Dipper. In other words, we might say that the North Star swings the Little Bear around by the tail.

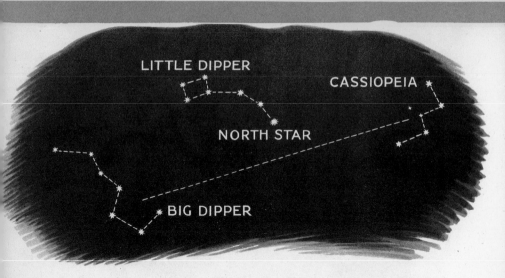

LITTLE DIPPER

CASSIOPEIA

NORTH STAR

BIG DIPPER

Straight across from the Big Dipper, on the opposite side of the North Star, is a group of stars in the shape of a W. This is the constellation Cassiopeia, or the Lady of the Chair.

If you prolong the line that connects the handle of the Big Dipper with the upper front star of the bowl of the Dipper, it will run into the constellation Auriga. The chief star of this constellation is the bright star Capella. Capella is 100 times larger and brighter than the sun.

If you prolong the line from the handle of the Big Dipper through the lower front star of the bowl, it will run into the constellation Gemini. Gemini is interesting because its two brightest stars are the Twins, Castor and Pollux.

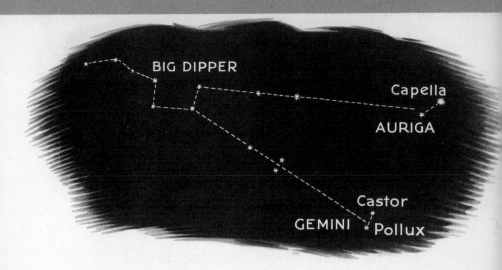

After you have learned this much about the stars of the northern sky, it will be a good idea to display your knowledge. Find someone else who would like to begin learning the constellations. Show him the Great Bear, the Little Bear, the North Star, Cassiopeia, Capella and the Twins. This will give you great satisfaction and will help you remember the stars better yourself.

If it is winter and we turn now toward the southern sky, we see the brightest of all constellations, Orion, the mighty Hunter. In the early evening, during February, Orion is almost directly south. He is about halfway between the horizon and the zenith, or point overhead.

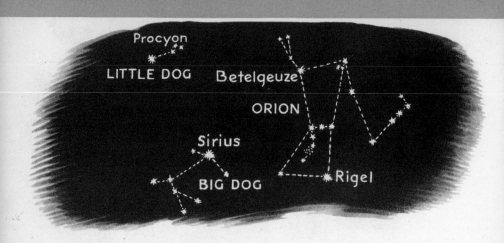

High above Orion near the zenith are the Twins. Following him closely is his faithful Big Dog, Canis Major, which contains Sirius, the brightest of all the stars. To Orion's left is a bright star, Procyon, which belongs to the constellation of the Little Dog, Canis Minor.

Below Orion's feet is the constellation of Lepus, the Hare, consisting of four stars arranged in the shape of a diamond. Facing Orion and the west is Taurus, the Bull with the gleaming eye. The eye of this Bull is the star Aldebaran. The Pleiades, or Seven Sisters, are also a part of Taurus, as are also the Hyades, a V-shaped group of stars, sometimes called the "rainy stars."

There are so many stories about Orion that

they often get mixed up by story tellers. One story is that Orion was originally a great hunter and also a great boaster. He boasted that there was no animal on earth that he could not defeat. The gods decided to punish him for being so conceited by causing a scorpion to bite his foot. Orion died from the effects of this bite, and both he and the scorpion were immediately placed in the sky. To keep the scorpion from biting Orion again, it was placed opposite Orion so that these two constellations are never above the horizon at the same time.

Another story is that Orion chased the Seven Sisters, or Pleiades, until Jupiter took pity on them and changed them into doves. The Pleiades were placed far enough ahead of Orion so that he would never be able to catch them.

Our Own and Other Galaxies

Every watcher of the sky can hardly have escaped seeing the hazy stream of light that stretches through the heavens on moonless nights when the sky is clear. Many know that this is the Milky Way, but few people realize that we live in it. The light of the Milky Way really comes from thousands of millions of stars too far away to be seen separately without a telescope. The stars of the Milky Way are arranged in the form of an enormous wheel. This whole wheel of stars is in slow rotation.

If we think of the Milky Way as an enormous wheel of stars, with the earth inside it, the stars will naturally appear closer together as we look toward the rim of this wheel. This is why the stars seem close together in some parts of the sky and scattered in others.

A disk-shaped group of stars such as the Milky Way is called a galaxy. In the Milky Way galaxy, the sun with its family of planets is about one third of the way up one of the spokes of the great wheel.

A GREAT DUST CLOUD IN THE MILKY WAY

In certain parts of the Milky Way there are dark rifts in the starry stream. These dark spots are great clouds of dust which cut off the light from the stars behind them. Probably the clouds contain many solid particles as well as dust.

Use a sky map to locate the constellation Andromeda. Within this constellation a hazy patch of light can often be seen. This patch of light is the Great Nebula in Andromeda. It is 800,000 light years away. This is the greatest distance that it is possible for us to see without a telescope—about five million million million miles.

For many years the Great Nebula in Andromeda was a puzzle to astronomers. It differed from the other objects they were able to observe with their telescopes. But when telescopes were built larger and larger, the form of the Nebula became clearer. It turned out to be a great spiral whirlpool of tens of thousands of millions of suns. It was another galaxy like the Milky Way.

Within recent years many other faraway galaxies have been brought into view by the giant telescopes. In the whole universe there are probably millions of them. But our own Milky Way galaxy so far seems to be the largest of all.

The vast spaces beyond the earth are rapidly being explored by more and more astronomers, using bigger and better telescopes. The largest telescopes can now pick up light from stars hundreds of millions of light years away, and reveal strange facts about these faraway points of light.

One of the strangest facts about the galaxies beyond the Milky Way is that they all seem

THE GREAT NEBULA IN ANDROMEDA

to be moving away from us. The farther away the galaxies are, the faster they seem to be moving away from the Milky Way galaxy.

What is the meaning of all this? So far, astronomers do not know. Some of them believe that we live near the center of an exploding universe, since all the galaxies seem to be rushing away from each other. How long will the universe keep exploding? Will the different galaxies ever rush back together again? Only time, long study and still bigger telescopes can ever help us find the answers to these questions.

Things to Do

1. Observe the sky on a clear night. Use sky maps to locate the brighter stars.
2. In reference books, look up the sizes of some of the stars, and their distances from the earth.
3. Make a list of first magnitude stars.
4. Construct a model of a variable star by making a bright object and a dark object revolve about a common center.
5. Read ancient legends about stars and constellations.
6. Make a sky map on a piece of dark paper. Punch holes with a pin to show the location of the brighter stars. Hold the map to the light, and use it to locate stars at night.
7. Make a small telescope.
8. Use opera glasses and field glasses to observe the stars.
9. Prepare reports on telescopes and discoveries made with telescopes.
10. Make a model of a constellation.
11. Take pictures of star trails.

Topics for Further Study

1. Astrolabe
2. Betelguese
3. Capella
4. Double stars
5. Galaxies
6. Galileo
7. Leonids
8. Herschel
9. Kepler
10. Light years
11. Milky Way
12. Multiple stars
13. Reflecting tele-scopes
14. Refracting tele-scopes
15. Star clusters
16. Star time
17. Sun
18. Tycho Brahe
19. Variable stars
20. Vega

In each of the groups of words below, select the word that includes the two other words in each group:

1. galaxy   stars   constellations
2. observatory   telescope   lens
3. Pleiades   Hyades   Taurus
4. Milky Way   Earth   Capella
5. Gemini   Castor   Pollux
6. Sun   Pluto   solar system
7. universe   galaxies   stars

Questions

1. How many miles are there in one light year?
2. What is the difference between a star and a planet?
3. Name six stars.
4. Name six constellations.
5. What is the difference between a reflecting telescope and a refracting telescope?
6. How do constellations help us locate single stars?
7. Why do the stars seem to rise and set?
8. Why is it necessary for telescopes to be moved by clockwork?
9. Why do many stars have Arabian names?
10. What is the zenith?
11. What is the real shape of the Milky Way galaxy?
12. What is the position of the solar system in the Milky Way galaxy?
13. How far can we see without a telescope?
14. What evidence do astronomers have that the universe is exploding?

THE IMPROVEMENT OF
PLANTS AND ANIMALS

Early Plant Breeders

Man has always depended upon plants and animals for food, shelter and clothing. For a long time he took what nature furnished him. But as time went on, man became dissatisfied with what he got from nature and began making improvements. Slowly he learned to plant the seeds of plants that he found most useful and to capture useful animals and tame them.

No one knows how agriculture began, but it may be interesting to make a few guesses. From the very earliest times people must have used fruits and seeds for food. Some of these were eaten where they were found, while some were brought to the camp or cave to be shared by others. Many of the seeds must have been dropped on the ground around the camp. Thus, without knowing it, the people of long ago collected the seeds of certain plants, and planted them close together.

Though the people of very early times ate many kinds of plants, they lived largely by hunting. When the game in one place became scarce, the people moved on. But sometimes they may have returned to the same camp site again and again. Imagine these early men returning to an old camp site after a year's absence. How surprised they must have been to find grain growing where they had dropped the seeds the year before.

There was one kind of wild grass that bore many seeds at the tops of its long stems. It was wheat. Why not grow wheat in a field instead of searching for it far and near? This idea came to some thoughtful man many thousands of years ago. When he tried out his idea and found that it worked, other people began to raise wheat, too.

One of the early wheat-growing peoples were the Lake Dwellers of Switzerland. These people built their houses over water. They were set on high poles near the shores of lakes. Wheat was grown in fields near the lakes.

Other kinds of wild grasses came to be cultivated very early in different parts of the world. Rice was probably first grown in China where it is still the main food of the people. Barley is another ancient crop. About five thousand years ago, before silver and copper came into use, barley was used as money. Rye was raised in northern regions where it was too cold for other grains. In the Americas, corn was the main crop. Pictures of corn, carved on clay dishes, have been found in the ruins of cities built many thousands of years ago.

Soon after men learned to plant seeds and grow crops, they began to make some other

important discoveries. Some of the plants they grew produced more food than others. Some tasted better than others and some kept better than others. The early farmers learned to select the better kinds and to save the seeds of these for planting. In this way they began the improvement of plants and became plant breeders.

Besides the grains, other plants gradually came into cultivation. Orchards of wild apples, wild cherries, wild oranges and wild peaches were planted. As time went on, these fruits were slowly improved by selection. Seeds of the better fruits were saved for planting, and the quality was further improved by cultivation.

All of the garden vegetables we raise today
are the result of thousands of years of plant
breeding. Many of them bear little resemblance
to the wild plants from which they came. As
an example, the wild cabbage is of little value
as a vegetable. Yet it is the ancestor of a large
family of excellent vegetables: head cabbage,
cauliflower, kohlrabi, kale and Brussels sprouts.
These plants differ widely in appearance and
in habits of growth. The differences were
brought about a little at a time by careful selection and breeding. But the fact that they all
have the same odor when cooked shows that
they really belong to the same family of plants.

Domestication and Improvement of Animals

From the earliest times, man has used animals as sources of food and clothing. At first, he hunted these animals, but gradually he found that some of them were easy to tame. He learned that it was less trouble to raise animals in captivity than it was to capture or kill wild animals. Still later, he discovered that animals could be used to help cultivate the soil and to do other kinds of work. When early man tamed animals for his use, he is said to have domesticated them. Civilization could never have developed without the aid of domestic animals.

There is little doubt that the wolf was the first animal to be domesticated. Probably this came about through the capture of wolf puppies. Raised in captivity, wolf puppies were tamed and became fond of man's company. The dogs we have today are all descendants of the common wolf of Europe. Through thousands of years, selection and breeding have produced various types of dogs.

Aurochs

The early ancestors of our cattle were fierce creatures called aurochs. The early inhabitants of Europe hunted aurochs for food, and sometimes they captured the calves and tamed them. Auroch calves raised in captivity grew up into animals less wild than their parents. By taming animals, gradually more and more people became herdsmen instead of hunters and thus changed their way of making a living.

Scottish Highland Cattle

In various parts of the world other useful animals were captured and tamed. The wild goat of Persia was domesticated very early, and goat-raising spread to many countries. Long before the time of recorded history, the ancient Egyptians kept goats, as did the Swiss Lake Dwellers.

The domestication of sheep took place so long ago that today they have no close wild relatives. There are wild sheep today, but they all have hair instead of wool, and long tails instead of short tails. But probably the first domestic sheep had hair and short tails. Possibly some shepherd of long ago noticed that one of the lambs from his hairy sheep had wool instead of hair. This single woolly sheep may be the ancestor of all the woolly sheep of today. All modern breeds of domestic sheep have long tails. Their tails are usually cut short when the lambs are a few weeks old.

Many kinds of deer have long been kept in parks, but the only kind that has been domesticated is the reindeer. Reindeer are still the most useful domesticated animals in northern Norway, Lapland and Siberia. They are strong animals, able to draw heavy loads hundreds of miles over the snow. Their milk and flesh are used for food, and their skins for clothing. In North America, reindeer are known as caribou.

The camel is one of the most valuable domestic animals in the hot, sandy regions of both Africa and Asia. The shape of its feet enables it to travel easily over soft sand. The food and water stored in its body enable it to go for days without eating or drinking. It is also able to close its nostrils during sandstorms.

In South America, the llama and alpaca were domesticated in very ancient times by the Indians. Male llamas were used as beasts of burden, and females provided milk and meat.

Alpaca   Llama

The hair of both males and females was made into cloth. The alpaca was useful only for its wool. Large herds of these animals are still kept for this purpose.

Horses are still wild animals in the desert regions of northeastern Africa. Herds of wild horses also exist in America and Australia, but these are descendants of domesticated horses that escaped and became wild again. Since most wild horses are easily tamed when captured, it is probable that the first domestication was not very difficult.

Wild Horse (Asia)

Since very ancient times, elephants have been tamed and trained to do useful work. Of all the animals, the elephant is one of the easiest to domesticate. In fact, it is much less trouble to capture and train elephants than to raise them in captivity. Nearly all elephants now in captivity were caught as wild animals.

Wild pigs have lived on the earth for several million years. A Chinese scholar has estimated that swine were first domesticated in China about 5000 years ago. Since that time, they have slowly been improved, and many different breeds or varieties have been produced.

Jungle Fowl

Certain birds were domesticated by man at a very early period. The wild ancestor of our chickens is the red jungle fowl of India. Chickens have been raised in captivity for more than 3500 years.

(male)

Domestic geese are descended from the Grey Lag goose which may still be found in the wild state in Scotland. Most kinds of ducks were bred from the wild mallard duck. The only domestic bird which comes from America is the turkey, a native of Mexico.

Several kinds of insects have long served man as domesticated animals. The best known of *(female)* these are probably the honeybee and the silk-
Lac Insect worm. Less well known is the cochineal insect, which produces a valuable dye, and the lac insect. The lac insect is carefully cultivated in the Far East. It produces a substance from which shellac and lacquers are made.

Modern Developments in Animal Breeding

During the thousands of years since man first began to domesticate animals, he has worked to produce kinds of animals which would be better suited to his needs. If we could compare the best domestic animals of today with the best animals of a thousand years ago, it would be clear that man has succeeded very well in this task. Cows give several times as much milk as they did a thousand years ago. The wool of sheep is now longer and of better quality. Pigs and beef cattle now produce more and better meat. Horses are faster and can pull heavier loads than those of many years ago.

Holstein Cow

Belgian Horse

The chief means of improving domestic animals is by selection. Man cannot create new kinds of animals. He can only improve the kinds he already has. Animals have within themselves the possibility of change. The animal breeder watches for these changes and selects animals for breeding which are best suited to his needs.

Just as no two people are ever exactly alike, so no two domestic animals are ever exactly alike. Animals differ in height, weight, shape of body, length of nose, color of hair and texture of hair, just as we do. In selecting animals

Shetland Pony

Guernsey Cow

that are to become the parents of other animals, breeders choose those that have the greatest number of good qualities and the fewest poor qualities.

It is well known that good qualities as well as bad qualities run in families. The offspring of two animal parents that have been selected for their good qualities are also likely to have these qualities. By selecting the best animals for parents and not allowing the poorer animals to become parents, breeders have succeeded in slowly improving our domestic animals.

Shropshire Sheep

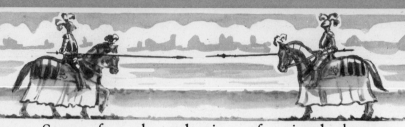

Soon after the selection of animals began, breeders discovered that it was impossible to get all of the desirable qualities they wanted in the same animals. In order to pull heavy loads, horses needed to be strong and heavy. But such horses could not travel very fast and were of no value as race horses. For this reason, horses began to be selected for special qualities. Some were bred entirely for speed, and others were bred entirely for carrying or pulling heavy loads. In this way, different varieties or breeds of horses were established.

The big draft horses of today are descended from the powerful war horses of ancient times. The knights had to have strong, heavy horses

Percheron

to carry their armor and coats of mail. When the methods of warfare changed, these big horses were raised for drawing heavy loads and doing farm work. From them still other breeds were developed in different countries: Shires in England, Percherons in France and Belgians in Belgium.

The Arabian horse was developed in Arabia. It is the ancestor of several of the modern breeds of race horses and saddle horses. George Washington rode an Arabian horse, as did Napoleon and other famous military leaders. Today, the outstanding horses that are bred for speed are the Standardbred, or American trotter, and the Kentucky saddle horse.

Arabian

Angus Cow

The two chief products of cattle are milk and beef. Long ago, breeders discovered that the cows that produced the most milk did not produce the best beef, nor did they get fat very easily. Cattle that did fatten easily and that produced good beef gave little milk. For this reason, most cattle are now bred for either milk or beef, but not for both.

Jersey Bull

Ayrshire Cow

Cattle breeders were not satisfied when they had produced dairy cattle that gave more milk than wild cattle did. By continued selection, cows were bred that produced more and more milk. The milk from the best cows was weighed after each milking, and records were kept. In this way, breeders could tell exactly which cows were the best milk producers. In Scotland men developed a breed called the Ayrshires, which

Jersey Cow

have long been noted for the quantity of milk they produce. In Northern Europe, another famous breed called Holsteins was developed. Both of these breeds of cattle are now widely raised in the United States. Some of the best cows have produced over 100 pounds, or fifty quarts of milk per day.

Cattle have also been selected for the quality of their milk. From the Island of Jersey, in the English Channel, comes the Jersey breed. From another island near by come the Guernseys. These cattle give milk very rich in butterfat. Several cows of these breeds have each produced enough milk to make 1000 pounds of butter in a year.

Besides horses and cows, other domestic animals have also been bred for special qualities. Some goats are bred for their hair, from which mohair is made, and others are bred for milk production. There are bacon-type hogs with

Light Brahmas *(meat)*   White Leghorns *(eggs)*

long bodies, and lard-type hogs with shorter, heavier bodies. There are heavy breeds of chickens raised for meat, and lighter breeds that are noted for their egg-laying ability.

In addition to selection, cross-breeding or hybridization is another method that has been used for the improvement of animals. Hybridization means the crossing of two animals that have somewhat different qualities. The offspring are called hybrids.

One of the most useful hybrid animals is the mule. The mule is a cross between a male donkey and a female horse. The advantage of this cross is that mules have most of the good qualities of both the donkey and the horse.

Some years ago another valuable hybrid animal was developed in Texas. Many of the good beef cattle of the Gulf region were dying of Texas fever. It was discovered that the humped cattle imported from India did not get this disease. When the Texas cattle and the cattle from India were crossed, the offspring had the desirable qualities of both breeds.

Sometimes, among many thousands of animals, one will appear that is different from all the others. For example, cattle without horns have appeared in several of the breeds. This lack of horns is an advantage, because it prevents animals from injuring each other when they fight. When hornless cattle become parents, the offspring are always hornless. A change of this kind is called a mutation.

Modern Developments in Plant Breeding

About forty years ago, the trailing habit and glossy foliage of a wild rose imported from Korea attracted the attention of a young gardener. He imagined how beautiful this rose would be if it bore flowers like those of other garden roses instead of clusters of small, white single flowers. He crossed this rose with garden roses and waited.

Three years later, his first crop of hybrid seedlings came into bloom. Among them were four plants that resembled the rambler rose; they bore flowers that resembled the garden roses. They were different from all other roses in the world. From these hybrids the gardener developed the famous Dorothy Perkins rose, which is so much admired and so widely cultivated in northern gardens.

The story of the development of the Dorothy Perkins rose is similar to that of many of the other improved plants grown today. In the breeding of plants the same general methods are used as in the breeding of animals. Selection, introduction and hybridization have all been employed successfully by plant breeders in the improvement of thousands of kinds of plants.

The simplest method of improving plants is by selection. The plant breeder selects a plant which has desirable characteristics and saves its seed. From that seed he grows plants which he again subjects to selection. He saves the seeds of these, taking advantage of whatever desirable variations happen to appear.

Several years ago, in a huge field of yellow poppies, Luther Burbank, a famous plant breeder, discovered a single flower with a thin red line upon one of its petals. He removed this plant and saved the seeds. From these seeds he grew many plants, some of which bore the same red line. Discarding the yellow types and sowing only the seeds of those that had a touch

of red, he found that the red line grew broader and broader with each new generation. Finally, it spread all the way across the petals, and a new red variety of poppies was created.

Patient selection of this kind has been responsible for most of the improvement that has taken place in flowers and food plants. This is the same method that was used by the early plant breeders. Recently more careful and scientific methods have been developed, and the improvement of plants has been speeded up greatly.

In some ways the problems of plant breeders are much more difficult than those of animal breeders. It is difficult to keep track of the parentage of plants that are pollinated by insects. Bees may bring pollen from a desirable plant or from an undesirable plant. Wind also blows pollen about from place to place.

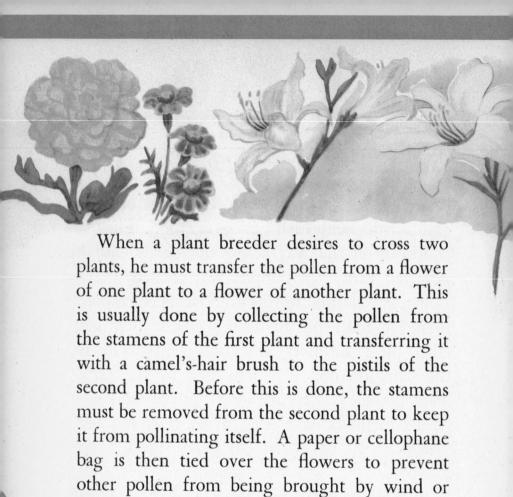

When a plant breeder desires to cross two plants, he must transfer the pollen from a flower of one plant to a flower of another plant. This is usually done by collecting the pollen from the stamens of the first plant and transferring it with a camel's-hair brush to the pistils of the second plant. Before this is done, the stamens must be removed from the second plant to keep it from pollinating itself. A paper or cellophane bag is then tied over the flowers to prevent other pollen from being brought by wind or insects.

Occasionally a new kind of plant appears that

is not the result of selection and breeding. In 1910 a red sunflower was discovered in Colorado. Seeds from this plant were grown, and all the offspring had red flowers. This showed that the red sunflower was a mutation. The red sunflower appeared suddenly just as cattle without horns did. Red sweet potatoes, seedless oranges and many other useful plants also began as mutations. Recently, scientists have found several ways of bringing about mutations by artificial means. One way is by placing seeds in the path of X rays for a short time. Another way is by the use of chemicals.

If a new or old variety of plants multiplies by seed, continued selection is necessary to maintain its standard. Without continued selection any variety of plants will begin to lose its good qualities. The same thing happens with domestic animals that escape and become wild again.

In plants that have woody stems, new varieties can be continued indefinitely in a very simple way. Twigs from a known variety of fruit may be made to grow on a tree that produces fruit of no value. The branches that grow from these twigs will bear fruit like that of the trees from which they came. When these branches become large enough, the original branches can be cut off. This process is known as grafting.

Steps in Grafting

New Varieties of Plants

What fun it is to go through the catalogs, look at the pictures and read the description of the flowers, fruits and vegetables! Then comes the difficult problem of selecting plants wanted, for there are many hundreds from which to choose. The first settlers had no such fun or problem. They found in all of what is now the United States approximately a dozen native food plants that are still grown today. Among these were corn, potatoes, tobacco, crab apples, tomatoes, squash, pumpkin, raspberries, beans and pecans. Of course, the early settlers brought the seeds of some other plants from their own homelands.

In 1827, when John Quincy Adams was President, he directed the American consuls abroad to send home seeds and plants which they believed could be grown profitably in America.

Cranberry

Since then, 96,000 plants have been introduced into the United States from all parts of the world. A branch of our Department of Agriculture, called the Division of Foreign Plant Introduction, has charge of this work. Each year this Department spends about $200,000 in sending plant hunters to all parts of the world. Many of the plants that they have introduced into our country have been raised successfully. The soybean, which was brought from the Far East, is one of our large crops. It is used for human food, animal food, oil, raw material for plastics and to enrich the soil. It is estimated that over $100,000,000 worth of soybeans are raised in the United States each year.

But plant hunters alone are not responsible for all of the many varieties of things that are grown in our country. The scientists who have stayed at home and worked patiently have developed hundreds of new things. They have looked for the unusual things; then by carefully selecting seeds and planting and replanting them, they have developed new fruits, vegetables and flowers. Our double, sweet-scented nasturtiums came from one tiny plant found in a little garden in Mexico. Golden bantam corn, a favorite variety for our roasts and picnics, came from a single ear that was discovered to be sweeter than others.

Many years ago in Brazil, a tree that bore seedless oranges was found. Of course, seeds from these oranges could not be planted because there were none. But, by grafting a branch that bore seedless oranges to an ordinary orange tree, other seedless oranges could be grown. By repeating this process, seedless oranges have been grown in thousands of orchards.

Sometimes several varieties of a fruit are raised on the same tree. A Long Island man has succeeded in making a single tree produce forty-seven kinds of apples and seven kinds of pears. Imagine one tree bearing red, yellow and green apples, sweet and sour apples, early and late apples!

During the past few years, scientists have learned to improve ordinary varieties of plants by the use of a chemical called colchicine. With this chemical, the wheat plant has been improved; it yields more wheat, grows in colder climates and better resists disease. Cotton has been raised with a longer and smoother fiber than formerly. Such fibers are easy to weave. Roses are produced with larger buds and blossoms than ever before. Marigolds now grow to be twice the usual size. They last a long time when put in water.

"One fourth of all the varieties of fruits and vegetables used today were unknown ten years ago," says one plant scientist. Indeed, almost every time we go to the fruit or vegetable store, we can find something new to buy. Many times we wonder whether we would like some of the unfamiliar things we see listed on menus.

Citrange   Limequat

Nectarine

Boysenberry

The newspapers and magazines tell of new fruits and vegetables recently developed. One is a fruit called the tangelo. It is a cross between a grapefruit and a tangerine. It looks like a small orange, but peels easily and has a distinctly new flavor. The citrange is another new fruit. It has been developed from the grapefruit. The topeppo, which is part tomato and part pepper, is little known. It is likely that the garlian, which is part garlic and part onion, will soon find its way into our soups and salads.

The boysenberry, although not quite so new as some fruits, is gradually becoming known, for it can be bought in cans. The boysenberry is a result of crossing the blackberry, loganberry and raspberry.

Instead of small, rough carrots with little color, we now have long, thin ones that are

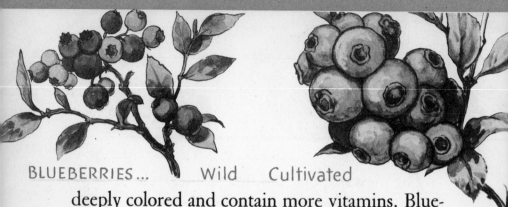

BLUEBERRIES...   Wild   Cultivated

deeply colored and contain more vitamins. Blueberries, which are usually so small that picking them is a tedious task, are now made to grow as large as an inch in diameter. Fuzzless peaches, eyeless potatoes, seedless watermelons and odorless cabbage have also appeared on the market.

With scientists finding new plants, developing new plants and producing new and improved varieties of those we already have, we may wonder what the seed catalogues and gardens of the future will show. With better and faster transportation, it is difficult to tell what will soon be in our stores. With new ways of canning and freezing foods, we may well wonder what next will be brought to us from other parts of the world. Although many remarkable things have been done in the past by plant breeding, many more are in store for the future.

New Breeds of Animals

During recent years scientists have been bringing about changes in the animal kingdom, just as they have been bringing about changes in the plant kingdom. Results that might have required nature thousands of years to accomplish have been brought about within a few generations.

One of the most interesting experiments in animal breeding was begun over fifty years ago by Dr. Alexander Graham Bell, the inventor of the telephone. During the summer of 1886, Dr. Bell took his family to Nova Scotia. To amuse his children he bought a sheep which he intended to sell in the fall. But when the sheep had a lamb, Dr. Bell's children persuaded him not to sell it.

But why should sheep have only one lamb at a time, Dr. Bell asked himself one day.

Hogs produce a dozen or more offspring at a time, and half a dozen puppies or kittens often arrive together.

After Dr. Bell had thought this over, he passed the word around to his neighbors that he would pay high prices for sheep that produced two or more young at a time. The first year he bought sixteen animals. He invented a system of ear punching so that he could keep complete records of his animals.

Dr. Bell continued his experiment for twenty-seven years. Since his death the experiment has been carried on by the University of New Hampshire, where, at the present time, about 70 per cent of the female sheep have twins. Occasionally, there are triplets.

Several long-range experiments are also under way by breeders of dogs. Most of the present breeds of dogs have been selected on the basis of physical qualities. Great Danes and other large breeds have been bred for great size. Toy dogs, of many kinds, are bred for small size. Others are bred for qualities that help to win prizes at dog shows.

English Bulldog

French Poodle

Experiments are now being carried on to find out how to breed dogs for mental qualities such as intelligence, friendliness and aggressiveness. In order to find out which dogs are most intelligent, ways have been found to give them intelligence tests. The dogs that get the highest scores on these tests are selected for breeding. Within twenty years, scientists hope to produce dogs that will be greatly superior to the dogs of today in intelligence and other mental qualities.

Chantecler chickens

Certain animals are now bred to meet definite requirements in somewhat the same way that buildings are constructed: according to a set of plans. In Canada, a breed of chickens was needed which would thrive in the cold climate. In 1908, a chicken breeder set out to produce such a breed. Special qualities found in five different breeds were combined, and a new breed was produced. The new breed had very heavy plumage, and very small combs which did not freeze even in the coldest weather. This new breed is now called the Chantecler. New breeds of other domestic fowls have been produced in a similar way.

Guinea fowl

Pekin duck

Another example of the breeding of animals to order is the recent development of "streamlined" turkeys. A type of turkey was needed which would fit into the small ovens of modern cook stoves. The U. S. Department of Agriculture set out to produce such a turkey by combining certain characteristics found in wild turkeys and in several domesticated types. Breeding stock is nearly ready for distribution to growers. The new turkey will be white, with compact body, short legs, and a long breast bone with plenty of white meat. It will mature in about 24 weeks. The hens will weigh from 6½ to 9 pounds when dressed, and the toms from 11 to 15 pounds.

Things to Do

1. Write a story about someone who was shipwrecked or lost in the woods, and who had to get along without domestic plants and animals.
2. Make a report on domestic animals found in other parts of the world.
3. Look up the history of common food plants such as wheat, corn and rice.
4. List important food plants that come from the New World and from the Old World. Which list is longer?
5. Make a list of different uses man has found for plants. Give examples of plants used for each purpose.
6. Find out about soil-less agriculture. Grow some plants without soil.
7. Visit a fruit or grocery store and find examples of new fruits and vegetables.
8. Make a report on domestic insects.
9. Practice grafting with twigs cut from trees. When you have learned to do it, graft some twigs on living trees.

10. Collect several kinds of pollen, and examine them under a microscope.
11. Report on the work of Burbank and other plant breeders.
12. Secure several seed catalogs, and find examples of new varieties of plants.
13. Visit a greenhouse.
14. Find out how vegetables are grown without soil.
15. Secure some U. S. Department of Agriculture bulletins on plant and animal breeding.

In each of the six lists below pick out the plant or animal that does not belong in each list.

1. cauliflower	kale	kohlrabi	onions
2. cabbage	rye	barley	corn
3. turkeys	chickens	goats	geese
4. honeybee	mosquito	lac insect	silkworm
5. pigs	wolves	dogs	horses
6. Belgians	Percherons	Arabians	Jerseys

Match each of the animals listed below with the place from which it came:

1. alpaca 8.		1. Arabia
2. camel 4.		2. Asia
3. chicken 6.		3. Europe
4. dog 7.		4. Far East
5. goose 3.		5. India
6. lac insect 5.		6. Mexico
7. saddle horse 1.		7. Scotland
8. turkey 2.		8. South America

Name four of each of the following:

1. Domesticated birds
2. Domesticated mammals
3. Domesticated insects
4. Breeds of cattle
5. Breeds of horses
6. Ways in which plants are improved
7. New kinds of fruits
8. Kinds of grain
9. Animals used to do work
10. Descendants of wild cabbage

Making a Study Outline

Make an outline of this chapter. The outline might begin as follows:

A. Early plant breeders
   1. How men lived in early times
   2. The beginning of agriculture
   3. Grains and fruits of long ago
   4. The improvement of food plants
   5. The cabbage family

Topics for Further Study

1. Ancon sheep
2. Aurochs
3. Burbank
4. Cattalos
5. Carrier pigeons
6. Chemurgy
7. Cheese
8. Citrange
9. Coco-demer
10. Colchicine
11. Copra
12. Cormorants
13. Hemp
14. Lac insect
15. Lake dwellers
16. Oyster farming
17. Pedigrees
18. Sisal
19. Soil-less agriculture
20. Sugar beets
21. Sugar cane
22. Tomatoes
23. Tung oil
24. Zebu cattle

Questions

1. What different methods have been used to improve plants?
2. What government agency is especially interested in plant and animal breeding?
3. How do we know that kale and cauliflower belong to the same plant family?
4. What are aurochs?
5. Why are camels especially useful in hot countries as domestic animals? *They carry their own water — and never get thirsty.*
6. What insects have been domesticated, and how is each useful?
7. What is the origin of each of these: ducks, geese, chickens and turkeys?
8. What different methods have been used to improve domestic animals?
9. What are the principal breeds of horses and cattle today?
10. What are hybrids?
11. What is a mutation?
12. How is grafting done?
13. Name some new varieties of plants.
14. Name some new breeds of animals.

KEEPING FIT FOR WORK AND PLAY

Muscles and Health

After a long year in the same surroundings, we look forward to vacation time. The most healthful and enjoyable vacations are those we spend among new surroundings, at a camp in the mountains or at the seashore with plenty of fresh air, good food, sunlight and exercise. Such a vacation should fill us with new stores of energy and give us the feeling of glowing, radiant health.

A person who is in perfect health is often said to be in the "pink of condition." The rosy complexion of such a person comes from an abundance of red blood in the small blood tubes under the skin. There are then no dangerous bacteria giving off their poisons into the blood. Digestion and the other body processes are taking place without any disturbance.

A person who is in perfect health "feels well." This sense of good feeling is mainly due to what is called muscle tone. Since muscles make up more than half the total weight of the body, it is not surprising that the muscles have a great deal to do with the way we feel. In health, the muscles are always in a state of mild contraction, or tone. In this state, the muscle cells are always ready for whatever activity the brain may direct them to do.

When people become ill, they lose the muscle tone which keeps them feeling well during health. The muscles become soft and flabby during certain diseases. Other conditions may bring about too great a contraction of the muscles. When this happens, we call it nervous-

MUSCLE CELLS

ness, but this kind of nervousness really has nothing to do with the nerves. It is a result of holding the muscles too tense. This tires out the muscle cells and gives us an unpleasant feeling.

In order to keep the muscles healthy and in good condition, a certain amount of exercise is necessary. People who take no exercise usually have weak muscles and tire very easily. Often they become too fat, because the food they eat is stored in the body instead of being used for heat and energy.

The best kinds of exercise are those that bring the largest number of muscles into use. That is why swimming, walking and playing games such as basketball and football are such good forms of exercise. A boy whose only exercise consists of playing marbles may develop strong muscles in his thumb, but this will not help the other muscles of his body.

The building of strong muscles by exercise is of great help in improving the posture. It is easy for strong muscles to hold the body erect. Weak muscles let the shoulders drop and allow other parts of the body to fall into unnatural positions.

For most boys and girls, no special kinds of exercise are necessary. Bending exercises, arm-waving exercises and kicking exercises help to strengthen the muscles; but walking, swimming and playing games do this just as well and are a great deal more fun.

Too much exercise may be harmful instead of helpful to the muscles. In some athletic games, energy is used up faster than it can be restored by the body. This causes waste products to form in the muscles. These waste products act as a kind of poison and cause the tired feeling called fatigue.

Overexercise may also be harmful to the heart. Just as our arm muscles become larger through exercise, the heart may become enlarged if it has to work too hard. In later life, when we no longer take so much exercise, an enlarged heart may cause serious trouble.

Hard work or play should be followed by rest and sleep. The harder the work or play, the more rest and sleep are needed. Many games are divided into halves or quarters to provide rest during the game.

During sleep, the waste products in the muscles are carried away by the blood, and the worn-out muscle cells are repaired. Growth also takes place almost entirely while we are asleep. That is the reason why boys and girls need more sleep than adults do. In order to maintain the best conditions for growth and health, an eleven-year-old boy or girl should sleep about ten hours every night. Adults may need no more than six or eight hours of sleep, because they are no longer growing.

The Water Supply

Four things are necessary to sustain life: air, water, food and a suitable temperature. Of these, air is the easiest to obtain. Temperature can be regulated by heating and cooling devices, and by the wearing of suitable clothing. Food and water are the most difficult to obtain.

For those of us who live in villages or cities, the problem of securing water appears to be simple. It is only necessary to turn a faucet to have all the water we need. But suppose there were no faucets to turn!

Screw-type Faucet

Spring Self-Closing Faucet

Ball-type Faucet

If there were no faucets to turn, we might obtain water from the nearest river or ocean. However, river water is likely to contain impurities that make it unsafe to drink. Ocean water is too salty to drink. Besides, it would be a great deal of trouble to carry all the water we need from a river or ocean to our homes.

If there were no water faucets, we might obtain water by digging a well. But, in cities, so many impurities seep down through the ground that water from wells is unsafe to drink. Besides, if every family in a city had a well, so much water would be taken from the ground that all except the deepest wells would soon go dry.

A third possibility would be to collect rain water. We might catch the water that runs off the roofs of houses, or set out some pots and pans in the back yard and wait for rain.

But rain water is also far from pure. The air over cities contains dust, smoke, germs and other impurities. When it rains, these impurities come down with the raindrops. After a rain, the air smells fresh and clean.

The safe and plentiful water supply that we enjoy today is the result of many scientific discoveries. Cities of long ago had neither faucets nor sewers. History tells us of terrible plagues that often swept through these ancient cities, killing thousands of people. By providing water-supply systems and sewage systems, cities of today have become healthful places in which to live.

The source of the water supply of a city depends upon the location of the city. A city located along the seacoast usually obtains its water supply from rivers or lakes farther inland, where there are hills or mountains. It is often necessary to build dams across rivers to make artificial lakes or reservoirs. The water is carried to the city through large pipes, called conduits. Gravity causes the water to flow in the conduits.

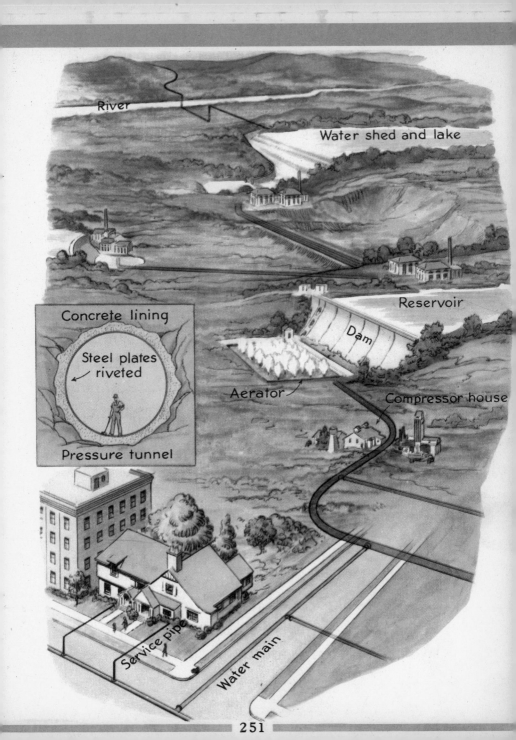

River

Water shed and lake

Reservoir

Concrete lining

Steel plates riveted

Dam

Pressure tunnel

Aerator

Compressor house

Service pipe

Water main

Pumping Station

Intake

Along the Great Lakes, most of the cities obtain their water directly from the lakes. Intake stations, called cribs, are built far out in the lake, where the water is purer than it is along the shore. Huge tunnels are dug to connect the cribs with the city. Pumping stations on the shore draw the water through the tunnels.

Many of the smaller cities obtain their water supply from deep wells. When rain falls on the ground, some of the water evaporates into the air and some of it runs into rivers, lakes or oceans. But some of it also sinks down into the ground. When this water reaches a layer of solid rock, it can sink no farther. Wells that reach down to these deep rock layers supply large quantities of water.

Water that is obtained from deep wells contains no dangerous germs. It is ready for use in homes. But water that is obtained from the surface of the ground often contains dangerous impurities. Surface water must be purified before it is ready for use.

The only way to remove nearly all the impurities from water is to distill it. Water is distilled by collecting and cooling the steam that comes from boiling water. The steam that comes off is pure water, and the impurities remain behind. This method is too slow and expensive to be used in purifying large quantities of water. In order to be safe for household use, however, water does not need to be absolutely pure.

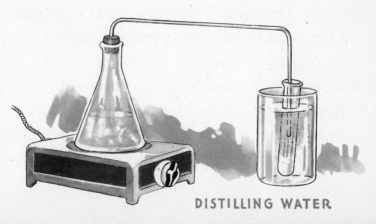

DISTILLING WATER

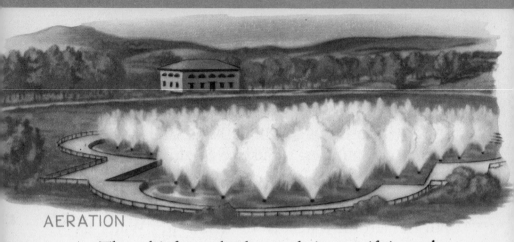

AERATION

The chief methods used in purifying the water supply of cities are: settling, aeration, filtration and the addition of chemicals. When water is allowed to stand in a reservoir for a week or two, most of the impurities settle to the bottom. Such water may be further purified by spraying it into the air. This brings the water in contact with the oxygen of the air, which helps to kill any germs that may be present. Sunlight also helps to kill germs.

Some cities find it necessary to filter their water. Large concrete tanks are built, and coarse gravel is placed in the bottom of them. A layer of fine gravel is added, then a layer of coarse sand and finally a layer of fine sand. The water to be purified is allowed to sink through these layers of sand and gravel. The impurities become lodged between the grains of sand, and clear water runs out at the bottom of the filter. Many cities also add a small amount of chlorine to their water supplies to kill any germs that have escaped the other processes of purification. Chemists make daily tests to find out how much chlorine should be added.

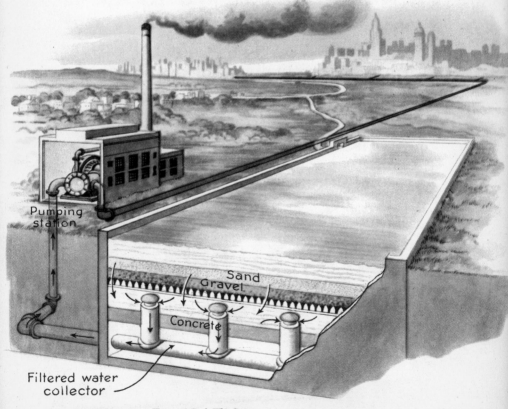

FILTRATION

Water is distributed to all the faucets of a city through a network of pipes. Large pipes, called water mains, run along under the important streets, and branches lead up the side streets. Still smaller branches lead into each house and building.

In planning the water supply system for a city, engineers figure that each person will use 100 gallons or more of water per day. In many cities, the average consumption of water is much more than 100 gallons per day for each person. Practically all of this water soon goes down the sewer. Another set of pipes must be provided to carry this waste water away. These pipes lead into large sewage mains which carry the wastes to sewage disposal

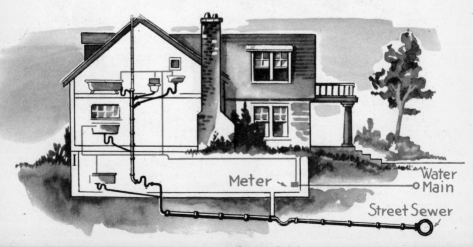

Meter ⌐

Water
o Main

Street Sewer

plants. There they are treated in various ways to make them harmless.

Though the amount of water we drink is very small in comparison with the amount used for other purposes, this amount is extremely important to our health. The foods we eat contain a considerable amount of water, but most people require at least six glasses of water daily in addition to this. Water is needed in the body to dissolve the digested foods and to help carry these foods to the cells. It is also needed to carry waste products away from the cells.

Over two thirds of the weight of our bodies consists of water. Our blood and our brains are about 90 per cent water. Muscles are about 50 per cent water, and even the bones contain about 30 per cent water. For the average person in good health, about a half gallon of water is excreted daily. Over one quart is excreted by the kidneys and about one pint each by the skin and the lungs. To make up for this loss, it is necessary to take a similar quantity of water into the body each day.

The Food Supply

One pound of coal contains more than enough energy to keep the body running for twenty-four hours. A half pint of gasoline would also be sufficient for our daily energy requirements. But, unfortunately, our bodies are not built to burn either coal or gasoline. Our supplies of energy must be obtained from foods.

The following quantities of different foods would each be sufficient to supply our energy requirements for one day:

Olive oil	1 pint
Sugar	2 pounds
Milk	1 gallon
Bananas	2 dozen
Beefsteak	2½ pounds

Even if a person happens to be very fond of one of these foods, it would be unwise to confine his diet to a single kind. Drinking a gallon of milk every day or eating two dozen bananas every day might make one quite uncomfortable. A diet consisting entirely of olive oil or beefsteak would probably be accompanied by indigestion. A person who ate nothing but sugar would soon lose his appetite for sugar.

In addition to the disadvantages mentioned, there are some other reasons why a diet consisting of a single kind of food, or even a few kinds of food, would be unhealthful. The body uses food not only to supply heat and energy, but also to furnish materials for growth, for repair of tissues and for the making of thousands of chemical substances used in the body. If only a few kinds of foods are eaten, some of the materials needed for good health are almost sure to be lacking. Sugar, for instance, contains no vitamins, minerals, fats or proteins. Beefsteak contains fats, proteins and some of the vitamins, but lacks carbohydrates and other necessary vitamins. In order to maintain perfect health, it is necessary for us to eat many different kinds of food.

Chemicals in the body of 150 lb. man

WATER 98 lb.

PROTEIN 22 lb.

FAT 20 lb.

SALTS 7½ lb.

SUGAR 2½ lb.

A few people have the strange notion that some kinds of food are not good to eat. For instance, some people do not like fish, while others enjoy it very much. It happens that fish are one of the best sources of iodine, which is essential to good health. The same people may not like cabbage either, possibly because someone has told them that it is not good to eat. Cabbage, cauliflower and all the rest of the cabbage family are among the best sources of calcium. Calcium is necessary for the building of strong bones and teeth. From these examples, it is easy to see how notions regarding foods may injure one's health.

Many cereals and other food products are now advertised in newspapers, in magazines and over the radio. Some manufacturers of breakfast foods claim that their products contain

Foods containing calcium

Which is better?

special energy-giving vitamins. Some manufacturers say that hot cereals are better than cold cereals. Some say that cold cereals are better than hot cereals. Sometimes famous baseball players and other athletes are paid to recommend foods. It is very interesting to make a collection of food advertisements and to compare the different claims that are made in each one.

The daily amount of food required to maintain good health depends upon several factors. Growing boys and girls require more food in proportion to their weight than adults do. Exercise and the season of the year also affect food requirements. Unless it has been already spoiled by bad food habits, the appetite is of some value as a guide in determining the kinds and amounts of the food we require.

PROTEIN →3½%
FAT →3½%
→5%
CARBOHYDRATES
MINERAL SALTS →1%

WATER 87%

Although no two people are exactly alike in their food needs, a few simple rules about eating should be kept in mind by everyone. "Drink a quart of milk every day" is a good rule to follow, unless there is some special reason for not drinking milk. Milk contains easily digested proteins, fats and carbohydrates, as well as plenty of valuable vitamins and minerals.

Two generous servings of vegetables should be eaten every day, one of which should be a leafy vegetable. Leafy vegetables are rich in minerals. Two kinds of fruit should also be eaten every day, one of them a raw fruit. Cooking destroys some of the vitamins that raw fruits contain.

Two foods rich in protein should be eaten every day. Proteins are necessary for growth and the repair of tissues. Fats and sugars should be eaten sparingly, because too large quantities of them tend to overwork certain organs of the body.

Ailments and Diseases

In any community, out of every 100 persons, 10 will be sick and 10 will be really well. The other 80 will be somewhere between these two extremes. They will not be sick nor will they be entirely well. When something is wrong with the body, there is always a cause. Practically everyone is born healthy, and ill health is usually the result of carelessness or ignorance.

When we have a toothache, we feel very uncomfortable, and enjoy neither work nor play. Each of our teeth has a hard outer part composed of mineral matter, and a soft inner part that contains nerves and blood vessels. If the outer part of a tooth decays, the nerves on the inside are exposed to the air. Then the tooth begins to ache.

Enamel —
Dentine —
Pulp —
Cement —

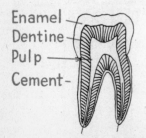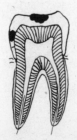

Strange as it may seem, improper food is often the cause of toothache. When a child is born, the teeth are hidden within the soft gums of the mouth. Food rich in certain minerals and vitamins is needed to make the outer parts of the teeth grow firm and hard. If the food does not contain enough of these minerals and vitamins, the teeth become soft and decay easily.

Most headaches and stomach-aches are also caused by improper food and eating habits. Some foods tend to pass through the intestines easily and rapidly. Others tend to move slowly and cause constipation. When food substances remain too long in the intestines, poisonous waste products are formed. These poisons may then enter the blood and cause a headache. A clogged intestine also interferes with the emptying of the stomach and results in stomach-ache. Constipation can usually be prevented by the selection of a mixed diet including plenty of fruits, vegetables and cereals.

Such ailments as toothache, headache and stomach-ache are usually not serious if they are

Bacteria
that cause
Tuberculosis

treated promptly. Permanent injury to the body is not likely to result if the conditions which cause these aches are quickly remedied. Most of the really serious troubles of the body are caused by bacteria and other very small living things.

One of the most dangerous kinds of bacteria is the kind that causes tuberculosis. This disease results from the growth in the body of tiny rod-shaped bacteria. The favorite place in the body for these bacteria to live is in the lungs; but they may also live in the bones, joints and other places.

Children never have tuberculosis when they are born, but later they may get the bacteria of tuberculosis from a person that has the disease. A person who has tuberculosis may cough or sneeze, and so spray the bacteria into the air. A well person may breathe in the bacteria

and get the disease. Cows also sometimes have tuberculosis. If they have, the bacteria are in the milk. Today, cows are usually tested to find out whether or not they have tuberculosis. One should always be careful to drink milk that comes from healthy cows.

Typhoid fever is caused by another kind of bacteria. This disease is often spread by milk which has been handled by someone who has the disease. Or it may be spread by water that contains body waste of someone who is sick with typhoid fever. Within the last few years, we have become more careful in keeping typhoid bacteria out of our milk and water supplies. Thus the disease has become much less common. Typhoid fever may also be prevented by certain medicines. These medicines are forced directly into the blood through a hollow needle.

The bacteria that cause diphtheria are usually present in the air near anyone who is sick with the disease. They are also likely to be found on articles that such a person has used or touched. For this reason, people who have diphtheria are quarantined, that is, kept away from other people so that the disease will not

spread. Diphtheria may also be prevented by the use of a medicine called toxoid. A person who has had the right amount of toxoid forced into his blood through a hollow needle cannot get diphtheria.

The most common of all diseases are colds. For a long time, scientists have been trying to discover the causes of colds, but they have only partially succeeded. When we have a cold, many kinds of bacteria are found in the nose, mouth and throat. But the same bacteria are also found in the same places when we do not have a cold.

It is now believed that colds are caused by very small living things called viruses. Viruses are much smaller than bacteria. When we catch cold, the viruses start to grow on the

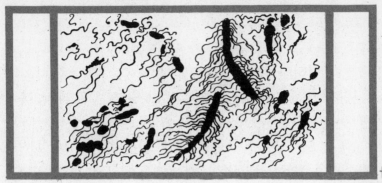

Bacteria
that cause
Typhoid fever

smooth linings of the mouth, nose and throat, and cause little breaks or openings in these smooth linings. Different kinds of bacteria then break through the linings and begin to grow. The growing bacteria then make the linings very sore, and give off poisons which make us feel sick.

One is more likely to catch cold in winter than in summer. When fall comes, people begin to spend much of their time indoors with the windows closed. If one person in a room sneezes or coughs because of a cold, others in the room are also likely to catch cold by breathing in little droplets that are sprayed into the air by sneezing.

A cough or sneeze should always be covered with a large handkerchief to prevent the little droplets from being sprayed into the air. When blowing the nose, it is best to hold the handkerchief a short distance away, and not to press on either nostril. If the nose is blown too hard, bacteria may be forced into the tubes that lead to the ear, and serious trouble may result.

Many medicines for the cure of colds are sold, but few of them work very well. The best way to cure a cold is to go to bed. Rest gives the body a chance to fight the harmful bacteria, and often prevents the more serious diseases that sometimes follow colds.

Besides helping to start colds, viruses also cause smallpox, measles, mumps, chickenpox, influenza and infantile paralysis. A few diseases are also caused by tiny animals too small to be seen without a microscope.

Animals that cause...

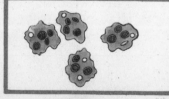

...Dysentery   ...Sleeping sickness

Things to Do

1. Survey the opportunities for recreation and exercise in your community.
2. Examine X-ray photographs of chest, teeth and bones.
3. Find statistics on the number of people injured or killed each year by accidents.
4. Discover methods for avoiding different kinds of accidents.
5. Study tables that give the nutrients, minerals and vitamins in different foods.
6. Keep a record of all the foods you eat in one day. Did you eat foods that contained all the necessary nutrients, minerals and vitamins?
7. Find out how certified milk is produced. What is grade A milk? Grade B milk? Pasteurized milk?
8. Make a list of the ways by which foods are kept from spoiling.
9. Study your local water supply system.
10. Read about the work of Pasteur, Trudeau, Von Behring, Jenner and Banting.

Complete the following statements:

1. The most beneficial kinds of exercise are those that

2. Overexercise may be harmful because

3. People who take no exercise usually

4. The best way to cure a cold is to

5. A city located along the seacoast usually obtains its water supply from

6. Over two thirds of the weight of our bodies consists of

7. Leafy vegetables are good sources of

8. Bones are connected to muscles by

9. Bones are connected to each other by

10. Most headaches and stomach-aches are caused by

11. Hard work or play should be followed by

12. Typhoid fever may be transmitted by

13. The only nutrient that sugar contains is

Make a list of each of the following:

1. Foods that are good sources of proteins
2. Foods that are good sources of fats
3. Foods that are good sources of carbohydrates
4. Foods that are good sources of minerals
5. Foods that are good sources of vitamins
6. Diseases that are caused by bacteria
7. Diseases that are caused by viruses
8. Diseases that are caused by animals
9. Methods used to purify water
10. Ways in which diseases may be prevented

Topics for Further Study

1. Alcohol
2. Bacteria
3. Baths
4. Blood
5. Brain
6. Cells
7. Drugs
8. Games
9. Glands
10. Liver
11. Lymph
12. Patent medicines
13. Poisons
14. Quarantine
15. Rickets
16. Shoes
17. Table manners
18. Tobacco
19. Vaccination
20. Vitamins

Questions

1. How is exercise important to health?
2. What is muscle tone?
3. Why are swimming, walking and playing games good forms of exercise?
4. How may overexercise be harmful?
5. Why do we need to sleep?
6. Describe several different methods used by cities to provide safe drinking water.
7. In what different ways may water be purified?
8. How much water should we drink each day and why?
9. For what different purposes does the body require food?
10. Why would eating a single kind of food be unhealthful?
11. Why do we need vitamins and minerals?
12. Describe several different ways in which diseases may be controlled.
13. What should each person do to protect himself and others from disease?
14. How can communities prevent disease?

TEACHING NOTES

Food for Growth and Energy, pp. 5-40

Problems:

  A. How do different animals secure food?
  B. What useful substances do foods contain?
  C. How do animals use food?

6–7. On the basis of careful observation it has been estimated that about 90 per cent of animal activity is consumed in the effort to secure food. Rocky Mountain goats are related to the chamois of Europe. In summer they usually feed on the sparse vegetation between the timber line and the snow line of high mountains. In winter they descend to lower altitudes. The puma, which eats mountain goats, is shown at the right.

8. Horses have both upper and lower biting teeth. Cows have no upper front teeth.

9. The great anteater has no teeth. Its only means of obtaining food is by the use of its long, sticky tongue.

10. Raccoons usually remain in tree tops during the day. At night they descend to feed.

12. An ameba has no definite shape. It is able to send out projections from any part of its body to engulf a particle of food.

14. A drop of pond water might contain all of the living things shown on this page. Both the plants and animals are magnified several hundred times. The animals all consist of a single cell.

15. The animals shown on this page consist of many cells but are too small to be seen without a microscope. Notice the beautiful colors and shapes of the tiny water plants.

17. The foods shown at the top are good sources of protein; those at the bottom are good sources of carbohydrates.

18. Top: foods rich in fat; bottom: foods rich in minerals.

21. The purpose of digestion is to make foods soluble so that they can pass from the alimentary canal into the blood. Sugar does not require digestion because it is already soluble.

22. A drop of blood contains about 5,000,000 red blood cells. The total number of cells in the body is in the trillions.

24. The average person has about five quarts of blood.

25. It has been estimated that if all the blood tubes in the body were connected in a straight line, they would reach to the moon.

27. Only the very largest blood tubes are shown. Pupils can use this diagram to trace the blood through the body.

33. Hot water should be used to make a thick sugar solution. A few small crystals may be attached to the end of a thread or string and should grow into larger crystals.

35. Bone cells remove minerals from the blood and deposit these minerals around themselves. The cells become prisoners within the bones.

38. *Proteins*—meat, eggs, beans.
  Fats—butter, peanuts, bacon.
  Carbohydrates—bread, sugar, potatoes.
  Minerals—cabbage, turnips, spinach.
  Vitamins—tomatoes, milk, cabbage.
  Water—watermelon, oranges, tomatoes.

Matching questions: Bats and mosquitoes. Flicker and ants. Gull and clams. Horse and grass. Raccoon and fish.

True or False: 1. False. 2. True. 3. True. 4. False. 5. True. 6. True.

39. Blanks: 1. Lungs. 2. Auricles. 3. Esophagus. 4. Arteries. 5. 98 or 99 degrees. 6. Tendons.

40. Answers: 1. Getting food. 2. By biting or pulling with teeth, tongue or mouth. 3. By dropping clams on rocks. 4. By straining food out of water. 5. By surrounding its food. 6. For heat, for energy and for growth and repair of tissues. 7. Mouth, esophagus, stomach, small intestines, large intestines. 8. To prepare food for absorption in the intestines. 9. Salivary, stomach and intestinal glands furnish chemicals which aid in digestion. 10. Cells are units of living matter. 11. From the blood. 12. Both produce heat and energy. 13. The body produces heat and energy in the cells. The body can grow and repair damaged or outworn parts. 14. Minerals and vitamins are chemicals necessary for the maintenance of good health. Minerals are especially necessary for bone tissues and other hard parts of the body. 15. By contracting, the muscles pull on the bones and move the body. 16. By enlarging cells and by adding more cells. 17. The blood carries heat to the skin where it can escape. The amount of blood going to the skin varies with the outside temperature. When we perspire, heat is taken away from the skin. This partly explains why the temperature of the body is always about the same.

Weather and Climate, pp. 41-80

Problems:
> *A.* What factors make up the weather?
> *B.* How are weather changes measured?
> *C.* How is the weather predicted?
> *D.* What changes in climate have taken place in the past?

42–43. Many improvements have been made recently in weather forecasting. Weather stations are being located at airports, where observations can be made by airplanes. Various kinds of weather balloons are also sent up at the airports.

44. The weather station on the top of Mt. Washington is shown in the illustration. Such stations supplement balloons in adding to our knowledge of upper air conditions.

46. With the air thermometer the direction of the rise and fall of the liquid in the tube will, of course, be opposite to that of the liquid thermometer. Placing the finger on the bulb of an ordinary thermometer will cause the liquid to rise in the tube.

47. The can experiment illustrates the principle of the aneroid barometer. In a mercurial barometer the space above the mercury is a vacuum, and the surface of the mercury at the bottom of the tube is exposed to the air. A rise or fall in air pressure causes a corresponding rise or fall in the height of the mercury.

48. In weather stations these and other weather instruments are placed on the roof. They are connected by electrical circuits to automatic recording instruments in a room below.

49. The weather recording instruments and broadcasting equipment attached to sounding balloons are illustrated. Automatic sounding balloons of this type have been in general use by the Weather Bureau since 1940. They are known as radio-sondes or ray sondes.

50. Even if it is not recovered, the cost of a radio-sonde is about the same as that of an airplane flight.

51. A teletype code has been devised which reports the location of the station, the barometric pressure, sky condition, humidity and temperature.

52. A recording barograph is shown in the foreground.

57. The rule for telling temperature by listening to crickets is usually accurate to within one degree.

58. The streaks in the sky sometimes referred to as "the sun drawing water" are rays of sunlight shining through holes in the clouds. Small droplets of water in the air make the rays visible in the same way that dust particles in a darkened room reveal the sun rays that may shine through holes in the shades.

61. Escaping steam is often seen moving upward through the air. Yet many people still hold the mistaken belief that moist air is heavier than dry air.

64. No two snowflakes are ever exactly alike.

65. The descending currents of air within a "high" move outward in a clockwise direction in the Northern Hemisphere.

66. The air moving into a "low" has a counterclockwise motion.

72. Orchard heaters are used when there is danger of frost in some orange groves.

73. The lowest official temperature reading is −90.4° F., in northern Siberia.

76. On the basis of the weather cycles of the past the climate for some years to come should be colder and rainier.

78. Correct answers: 1. Temperature. 2. Wind speed. 3. Air pressure. 4. Wind direction. 5. In layers. 6. Ice crystals. 7. Gale. 8. Hail. 9. Stratus clouds. 10. Cumulus clouds.

79. Blanks: 1. Meteorologists. 2. Hurricane. 3. Precipitation. 4. Red dust. 5. Climate. 6. Typhoons. 7. Rises. 8. Falls.

80. Answers: 1. It keeps them informed about weather conditions. 2. Large masses of air many miles wide that move across the earth's surface. 3. Because of the earth's rotation, winds blow toward the east. 4. Layers of ice form on frozen raindrops. 5. Whirling masses of air. 6. An enclosed liquid expands or contracts according to the amount of heat absorbed or released, thus registering temperature on a scale. 7. The revolving cups turn a speedometer apparatus which indicates the speed of the wind in miles per hour. 8. "Highs" and "lows" are areas of high or low air pressure. 9. Local showers are caused by rapidly rising clouds. 10. Superstitions are very unscientific explanations. 11. A theory is an explanation which has some basis in fact. 12. The higher the temperature, the faster crickets chirp. 13. Thermometers, barometers, anemometers, rain gauges, etc. 14. The Torrid Zone, the Temperate Zone, and the Frigid Zone. 15. Evidence from glaciers, fossils, and other evidence indicates changes in climate. 16. Dust cloud and land surface theories have been advanced to explain changes in climate.

Electricity and Its Uses, pp. 81-128

Problems:

A. How are electromagnets made?

B. How are messages sent by electricity?

C. How is electricity used to furnish heat and light?

D. Of what importance is electricity to modern living?

82-83. Bill wisely tried out his apparatus again and again to see whether it would work.

85. Caution. If you try Bill's apparatus, be sure that the electromagnet is strong, that the can and weight are evenly balanced and that the can is close enough to be pulled by the magnet.

87. Bell wire is insulated wire. The piece of iron in the center of the spool should be soft iron. Under similar conditions, a piece of steel would become a permanent magnet.

88. BB shot made of steel are better than tacks.

90. Be sure that the "long" piece of wire is long enough to make forty turns and to have ends left over to connect to the binding posts of a dry cell.

91. The early experimenters with electricity believed that a current traveled over a circuit from the positive pole to the negative pole. We now know that electrons travel from negative to positive as indicated by the arrows in the illustration. The spark was caused by a short circuit. Insulated wire is wire covered by a substance that is a poor conductor of electricity: rubber, silk, shellac, etc.

92. Another way to make a horseshoe electromagnet is to wrap insulated wire around a piece of soft iron wire, and then bend the wire in the shape of a horseshoe.

99. The "spurts" or variations in the flow of electric current affect the strength of the electromagnet, which, in turn, causes the disk to vibrate in such a way that the voice at the telephone transmitter is actually reproduced at the telephone receiver.

100. The type of antennae used to produce a bi-directional radio beam is shown at the left and that for a uni-directional beam at the right.

102. Heating "elements" are sometimes coils of wire and sometimes straight wires strung over some noncombustible material.

104. Tungsten filament lamp bulbs are now filled with a mixture of nitrogen and argon.

106. The nozzle of this turbine is made from the glass tube of a medicine dropper.

106. The ends of glass tubes are usually closed by heating in a very hot gas flame. High school science teachers or chemistry pupils should be willing to prepare such tubes.

A simpler bearing for this turbine can be made by pushing a short piece of glass tubing through a one-hole stopper so that the end of the tube is flush with the top of the stopper. A thumb tack can then be pushed into the stopper so that the circular part extends over and closes the top of the tube.

108. The illustration on page 109 will make clear the meaning of the term "penstock."

110. "Motion" really refers to mechanical energy. A generator or motor changes one form of energy into another.

118. Notice that the wire at the left is connected with all the lamps. Lamps numbered 3, 4, 9, and 11 are on one circuit; the caution lamps 5, 6, 7, and 8 are on another circuit and 1, 3, 10, and 12 are on a third circuit.

119. A strip of zinc for the electric cell may be obtained at a hardware store; sal ammoniac from a drugstore.

121. Note that Robert used two permanent magnets. He used the north pole of one and the south pole of the other for his motor. Betty's electric motor on page 110 had an electromagnetic field.

A motor of this kind can be built very easily. The ends of the permanent magnets that are nearest the armature should be opposite poles. Inexpensive kits containing plans and materials for the building of small motors are available in some stores.

122. The blinker shown in the picture is a flashlight bulb and a small porcelain socket.

123. The contact knobs on the question and answer board are ordinary paper fasteners. These are inserted in holes in the cardboard and connected with wire as shown. Different wire connections can be made for different sets of questions and answers.

124. The street lamps should be connected in parallel across the wires that run along the streets. Miniature porcelain sockets and flashlight bulbs are most convenient for these.

127. The buzzer shown may need to be adjusted to make it operate properly. This can be done by turning the screw.

True and false: 1. Insulated. 2. True. 3. True. 4. Electricity.

128. Match: Ocean cable and Field. Electric lamp and Edison. Electromagnet and Henry. Radio waves and Hertz. Telegraph and Morse. Telephone and Bell.

Answers: 1. By winding insulated wire around a soft iron core. 2. A bar magnet is a permanent magnet. An electromagnet is effective when a current of electricity flows in the coil of insulated wire. 3. By increasing the current, or by using more turns of wire with the same current. 4. Wire covered by a substance that is a poor conductor of electricity. 5. To prevent a short circuit and to cause the electric current to flow around and around the core. 6. Copper. 7. Soft iron. 8. Lighting, heating, running machines, etc.

The World of Sound, pp. 129-160

Problems:

A. What are sounds?
B. How do sounds differ?
C. How do sounds travel?
D. How do we hear sounds?

130-131. The distance between Buffalo and New York via the Erie Canal is about 450 miles. Since sound travels at the speed of about 12 miles per minute, the actual time required for the sound to travel this distance was about 38 minutes. The rest of the time was used up in firing the cannon. In 1825 this feat was regarded as a remarkable achievement in rapid communication.

132. Locate Krakatoa on a map.

133. A New York City subway train and station are illustrated.

134. The vocal cords are really not cords at all. They consist of two flaps of tissue with thin flexible edges. When they are drawn close together and the air is forced through them, they vibrate and produce sounds.

135. The saw can also be played by holding the handle between the feet as shown in the illustration. When swished through the air, the blackboard pointer disturbs the air particles and sets up sound waves.

136. The column of air within the tube vibrates. The shorter the tube, the higher the pitch of the sound.

137. Although air particles move back and forth, it is the wave that actually moves away from the vibrating body. This experiment illustrates the transmission of sound in a single plane. Actually sound waves are spherical and travel in all directions.

138. Men have longer vocal cords than women; hence their voices are lower.

139. The wavy grooves on a phonograph record cause the needle to vibrate. These vibrations are transmitted through the needle to a disk which causes air vibrations or sound waves.

142. A piece of copper tubing flattened at one end works very well. The test-tube pipe organ can also be operated by holding the lips in the right position and blowing across the tubes.

144. The term "strings" is used in the general sense. Wire strings are best for most experiments with sound.

145. In this case, the table top or door is also set in vibration. A sounding box is that portion of the musical instrument which vibrates in sympathy with the sound-producing part. In a banjo, it is principally the head. In a piano, it is probably the entire case.

149. In a tin-can telephone, the vibrations are transmitted along the string. In a real telephone, the vibrations do not travel through the wire, but cause variation in the electric current carried by the wire.

150. Echoes cause bad acoustics in auditoriums. Children will think of other observations which indicate that sound travels more slowly than light.

154. When a very loud sound is expected, keeping the mouth open will usually prevent damage to the eardrum.

155. Bats utter shrill cries while flying. These cries cannot be heard because their vibration rate is about 50,000 per second. Echoes from these cries enable bats to avoid running into obstacles.

156. The swelling of a hummingbird's throat in silent song is fairly easy to observe.

158. Correct word: 1. Echoes. 2. Second. 3. Air. 4. Pitch.

159. Principles: 1. B; 2. A; 3. A; 4. B; 5. C; 6. A; 7. C; 8. B.

160. Answers: 1. Sound is a sensation caused by vibrations. 2. Pitch describes the highness or lowness of a tone. 3. The movement of wings sets up air vibrations which cause a buzzing sound. 4. By tightening or loosening steel wires. 5. There is no air or other sound-conducting material between the earth and sun. 6. Pitch, loudness, quality. 7. By changing the length, by changing the tension, by changing the size or thickness of the strings. 8. Sound travels about 1000 feet per second in air, 5000 feet per second in water, and 16,000 feet per second in steel. 9. By vibrating vocal cords. 10. By changing the length of the vibrating strings with the use of the fingers. 11. By changing the length of the vibrating air-column. 12. Echoes are reflected sound waves. 13. By a very delicate organ, the ear. 14. To determine the presence and location of icebergs, etc. 15. When the sound sensation results from vibrations which do not harmonize pleasingly.

Wonders of the Sky, pp. 161-192

Problems:
  A. What is beyond our solar system?
  B. What are constellations?
  C. What is the nature of our galaxy?

162–163. Observatories are usually located some distance away from the glare of city lights. The larger ones are built on mountains where the air is clear and where there are few clouds. Beside the domes that house the telescopes, there must be rooms for the library, dark rooms for developing pictures, special laboratories and repair shops. Some large observatories have rising floors that are moved like elevators so that a person may stand or sit on a level with the eyepiece of the telescope.

164. Like the sun, the other stars are also in rapid motion. But their relative positions change very slightly because of their great distance from the earth.

165. Photographs of the great star cluster in Hercules, as well as other star clusters, can be found in many reference books.

166. Calculation of the number of miles in a light year and the distances in miles to certain stars will provide excellent practice in multiplication.

168. Stars appear to be no larger when seen through a telescope than they appear to the naked eye. The reason is that the stars are so far away that scarcely more than a single beam of light reaches us. The brightness of a star is no indication of its size. The nearest star is four light years away but it cannot be seen without a good telescope.

170. The largest successful refracting telescope has a lens 40 inches in diameter. Lenses cannot be made larger than this because their weight would pull them out of shape. The largest reflecting telescope, on Mt. Palomar, has a mirror 200 inches in diameter.

172. Stars can usually be seen in the daytime if the observer is at the bottom of a deep well or is looking through a tall chimney. Planets are often seen on clear days without a telescope.

174. In some cases, it may be possible to visit a planetarium.

176. The North Star is very near, though not exactly at the north celestial pole.

177. The umbrella, with a few constellations marked on the under surface in chalk, may be clamped to the globe bracket or simply held above the globe as the globe is rotated. To show the apparent motion of the stars, have pupils hold the umbrella and turn the handle slowly.

179. The North Star is not exactly at the north celestial pole; it therefore appears as an arc of light on star trail photographs. The trails shown represent about a six-hour exposure. The broken line seen in some of the trails was probably caused by a passing cloud. A list of the twenty stars of first magnitude, together with interesting data concerning them, can be found in many reference books.

180. Children imagine that they see the Dippers in almost every part of the sky. Usually it is possible to determine whether a boy or girl really sees the Big Dipper by inquiring in which direction the handle pointed at a given time of night and season of the year.

184. Most people can see only six of the Seven Sisters. A person with very good eyesight can see seven.

188. Many bright objects attached to a rotating wheel make a good model of a galaxy.

189. The shape of our own galaxy is similar to that of the Great Nebula in Andromeda.

191. Right words: 1. Galaxy. 2. Observatory. 3. Pleiades. 4. Milky Way. 5. Gemini. 6. Solar system. 7. Universe.

192. Answers: 1. 186,000 × 60 × 60 × 24 × 365. 2. A star is a sun and shines by its own light; a planet reflects light from the sun. 3. The North Star, Capella, Castor, Pollux, Aldebaran, Procyon. 4. Arian, Cassiopeia, Ursa Major, Gemini, Lepus, The Pleiades. 5. A reflecting telescope has a concave mirror instead of a lens at the base of the telescope. 6. If we can locate the constellations, their shape is a help in locating single stars. 7. Because of the rotation of the earth about its axis, the stars, like the sun, seem to rise and set. 8. Because of the rotation of the earth. 9. The Arabs were interested in stars and named many of them. 10. The zenith is a point in the sky directly overhead. 11. The Milky Way galaxy is shaped like a big thick wagon wheel. 12. The solar system is located about one third of the distance between the center and the edge of the Milky Way galaxy. 13. We can see the Great Nebula which is about 800,000 light years away. 14.

All the galaxies seem to be rushing away from each other just as particles in an exploding substance do.

The Improvement of Plants and Animals, pp. 193-240

Problems:
    A. What is the origin of our domestic plants and animals?
    B. How have plants and animals been improved?
    C. How do we get new varieties of plants and animals?

194-195. The improvement of plants and animals was already well advanced in Biblical times.

196. Wheat, rice, barley and rye are shown (left to right). Wheat is mentioned in some of the earliest written records. Grains of wheat have also been found in the pyramids of Egypt.

197. The Lake Dwellers had a highly developed culture. Their houses were probably built over water for protection and were connected with each other by little bridges. Drawbridges, which connected with the land, were pulled away from the shore at night.

199. The illustration shows corn culture by the Indians of Central America.

201. Scene in Scandinavia about 1300 A.D. The horses of this time were much smaller than the farm horses of today. The plow and other implements are characteristic of the period.

202. The European wolf is shown at the top. The dogs shown are the Irish setter (top left), and Dalmatian (top right). At the bottom (left to right) are a spaniel, Scottish terrier, Great Dane, and dachshund.

204. In some sheep the tails are adapted for the storage of fat. They become much thickened when food is plentiful and thinner when food is scarce.

207. Young wild pigs have stripes. As they become older, the stripes disappear.

208. Certain plants are grown to provide food for lac insects. The insects deposit a sticky substance on the twigs of these plants which, when removed and melted, becomes the shellac of commerce.

209. Breeders of dairy cattle keep accurate records of the amount of milk and butterfat produced by their animals. Those that produce the most are the most valuable for breeding.

213. Interesting books about horses are available in most libraries.

214. Beef cattle tend to store fat in their bodies while dairy cattle rarely become fat because of the large amount of milk they produce.

216. Some hogs weigh as much as 1000 pounds, as much as the average cow.

217. Mules are generally infertile and are always produced by hybridization.

218. Hornless cattle have now appeared in many of the breeds of modern cattle.

222. Top: Tetra marigold, hybrid French marigold and two varieties of day lilies. Bottom: Narcissus, jonquil, Shasta daisy.

223. Top: Petunias—Hollywood Star, giant fringed and Betsy Ross. Bottom: New spoon chrysanthemum, aster, scabiosa.

225. Cranberries are also one of our native food plants.

232. The smallest breed of dogs is the Mexican hairless, or Chihuahua.

234. Compare the combs of these Chantecler chickens with those of the other breeds.

235. Streamlined turkeys have already been marketed on a small scale.

237. Words that do not belong: 1. Onions. 2. Cabbage. 3. Goats. 4. Mosquito. 5. Wolves. 6. Jerseys.

238. Match: 1. Alpaca and South American. 2. Camel and Far East. 3. Chicken and Asia. 4. Dog and Europe. 5. Goose and Scotland. 6. Lac insect and India. 7. Saddle horse and Arabia. 8. Turkey and Mexico.

Four of each group: 1. Chickens, geese, turkeys, pigeons. 2. Cows, horses, sheep, goats. 3. Bees, lac insects, silkworms, cochineal. 4. Jersey, Hereford, Ayrshire, Holsteins. 5. Shires, Percherons, Belgians, Standard-bred. 6. By carefully selecting seeds, by crossing, by chemicals, by X rays. 7. Citrange, boysenberry, fuzzless peaches, tangelo. 8. Corn, wheat, rice, oats. 9. Oxen, dogs, camels, elephants. 10. Brussels sprouts, cauliflower, kohlrabi, kale.

240. Answers: 1. By selecting seeds from plants that show desirable characteristics, by cross pollination, by grafting, by the use of chemicals, X rays, etc. 2. The Department of Agriculture of our Federal Government, with headquarters in Washington, D. C. 3. The odor is one indication. 4. Aurochs were the ancestors of our cattle. 5. Camels can go long distances without food and water. 6. Bees for their honey, silkworms for silk, cochineal for dye, lac insect for shellac. 7. Ducks from wild mallards, geese from grey lag geese of type found in Scotland, chickens from red jungle fowl of Asia, turkeys from wild turkeys of Mexico and the southern part of the United States. 8. Animals have been improved by careful selection and breeding. The crossing of breeds and other methods are used. 9. The Standard-bred, Shires, Percherons, Belgians, Shetland—Hereford, Ayrshire, Holsteins, Jersey, Guernsey, etc. 10. Hybrids are the offspring of similar but different kinds of living things. 11. A mutation is a new type of animal or plant that suddenly appears. 12. Grafting is done by growing part of one plant on another plant. Seedless oranges, paper-shelled pecans and certain figs are grown on branches which were grafted on more common varieties of the same kind of plants. 13. Plants that produce the tangelo, the topeppo, the garlian, the boysenberry, eyeless potatoes, odorless cabbage, etc. 14. The Chantecler, "streamlined" turkeys, improved breeds of dogs, etc.

Keeping Fit for Work and Play, pp. 241-270

Problems:

A. How is exercise important to health?

B. How is water important to health?

C. How is a good water supply provided?

D. How are the proper kinds and amounts of food important to health?

E. How may certain ailments and diseases be prevented?

243–244. Many children do not have the opportunity to spend their vacations in the mountains or at the seashore. However, there are usually many opportunities for healthful recreation and exercise in the local community. A survey of the recreational facilities of the community should help children to become aware of the opportunities that exist.

245. Voluntary muscles are striped. Involuntary muscles are unstriped.

246. The relation of proper exercise to good posture cannot be overemphasized.

247. It is well known that overexercise often shortens the lives of athletes.

248. Children are surprised usually to discover that they are taller in the morning than they are in the evening. Careful measurements sometimes reveal a difference of as much as one-half inch. This is partly explained by

the fact that the weight of the body compresses the pads between the bones during the day. The fatigue of certain muscles may also make it impossible to assume a completely erect posture in the evening.

249. The operation of each of the three types of faucets shown will be apparent from a study of the diagrams.

251. This illustration will bear careful study and should provide a basis for considerable discussion. For instance, notice the way the conduit crosses the river shown at the top.

252. Some cities empty their sewage into the same lake from which they obtain their water supply. The water along the shore of such a lake is likely to be polluted. For this reason the conduits are sometimes run out into the lake for a distance of fifteen or twenty miles where the water is relatively free from dangerous impurities.

253. The distillation of water can be made more interesting by distilling muddy water. The soil particles remain behind because only water can change to steam. A cork stopper should be used because a rubber one will impart a disagreeable taste to the distilled water.

255. Sand filters are cleaned periodically by pumping water through them in the opposite direction.

259. The section in Unit 1 on "Useful Substances in Foods" should be reviewed at this point.

261. Critical reading of food advertisements will reveal many inconsistencies which amuse children. They may be left to draw their own conclusions with safety.

262. The drinking of milk sometimes becomes a fetish with children. In some cases forced diet of milk is harmful instead of helpful.

264. Improper food is a primary, though indirect, cause of tooth decay. There are, of course, many other causes.

268. Three major cold epidemics usually sweep across the United States each year. The first one starts late in September, the second arrives in February and the third in April.

269. More remedies for the treatment of colds are sold than for any other infection. Most of them are ineffective because the true nature of colds is not completely known. However, recent work on viruses increases the prospect of more effective methods of treatment.

272. Complete: 1. Involve the use of many muscles. 2. It may strain the heart. 3. Have weak muscles. 4. Rest. 5. Rivers or lakes. 6. Water. 7. Vitamins and minerals. 8. Tendons. 9. Ligaments. 10. Improper food and eating habits. 11. Rest. 12. Water or milk. 13. Carbohydrates.

273. Lists: *Sources of proteins:* Eggs, lean meat, peas, beans. *Sources of fats:* Milk, meat, nuts. *Sources of carbohydrates:* Potatoes, bread, fruits, root vegetables, etc. *Sources of minerals:* Meats, milk, cabbage, and other leafy vegetables. *Sources of vitamins:* Cod-liver oil, butter, fresh vegetables, etc. *Diseases caused by bacteria:* Tuberculosis, typhoid fever, diphtheria, etc. *Diseases caused by viruses:* Colds, smallpox, measles, mumps, chickenpox, influenza, infantile paralysis. *Diseases caused by animals:* Sleeping sickness, malaria, pork worm, hookworm. *Methods of purifying water:* Distillation, filtration, aeration, chemical. *Ways to prevent diseases:* Vaccination, injections for immunity, quarantines, antiseptics, etc.

274. Answers: 1. Exercise helps blood circulation, creates muscle tone and helps body function properly. 2. Muscle tone is that condition of the muscles that makes for a "well" feeling. 3. These exercises involve the use of the greatest possible number of muscles. 4. Overexercise may injure the

heart, cause waste materials to form in the muscles and cause fatigue. 5. Sleep is needed for growth, repair of tissues, elimination of waste products and for rest. 6. Safe drinking water is provided by filtering through gravel and sand, by aeration to permit oxygen to kill germs and by the use of chemicals, such as chlorine. 7. Water may be purified by methods described above, by boiling and by distillation. 8. Most people should drink about six glasses of water each day. We need water to dissolve our food, to help carry food to the cells, to help eliminate waste products and to carry on the normal functions of various parts of the body. 9. The body needs food for growth, for repair of tissues and for energy. 10. A single kind of food would not contain all the food elements needed for good health. 11. Minerals are needed especially for the teeth and bones. Vitamins are necessary for proper growth of tissues, for the prevention of certain diseases and for the proper functioning of the body. 12. Diseases may be controlled by killing the germs, by preventing the spread of germs, by building up resistance to germs, etc. Methods: purifying water, pasteurizing milk, cleaning the teeth and hands, efficient sewage disposal, refrigerating foods, vaccinations, toxoids, quarantines, etc.

INDEX

167/113